For Bruce and our time at
Chicago and our Modern Memoirs.

Harry

HISTORY'S DISQUIET

HISTORY'S DISQUIET

Modernity, Cultural Practice, and the Question
of Everyday Life

Harry Harootunian

The Wellek Library Lecture Series
at the University of California, Irvine

NEW YORK
COLUMBIA UNIVERSITY PRESS

Columbia University Press
Publishers Since 1893
New York   Chichester, West Sussex

Library of Congress Cataloging-in-Publication Data

Harootunian, Harry D., 1929–
   History's disquiet : modernity, cultural practice, and the question of everyday
life / Harry Harootunian.
      p. cm. — (The Wellek Library lecture series at the University of California,
Irvine)
   Includes bibliographical references and index.
   ISBN 0–231–11794–9 (cloth : alk. paper)
      1. Civilization, Modern—20th century.   2. Europe—Civilization—20th
century.   3. Japan—Civilization—20th century.   4. Postmodernism—Social
aspects.   5. Postcolonialism.   6. Europe—Intellectual life—20th century.
7. Japan—Intellectual life—20th century.   8. East and West.   9. Asia—Study
and teaching.   10. History, Modern—20th century—Philosophy.   I. Title.
II. Series.

CB427 .H28 2000
909.82—dc21   99–056305

EDITORIAL NOTE

The Wellek Library Lectures in Critical Theory are given annually at the University of California, Irvine, under the auspices of the Critical Theory Institute. The following lectures were given in May 1997.

The Critical Theory Institute
John Carlos Rowe, Director

For Holly, Claudia, and Jonathan, and the everydays
of their children Christine, Katherine, Patrick, Ani, and Andrew

Now as many times before, I am troubled by my own experience of my feelings, by my anguish simply to be feeling something, my disquiet simply at being here, my nostalgia for something never known. . . . And the light bursts serenely and perfectly forth from things, gilds them with a smiling, sad reality. The whole mystery of the world appears before my eyes sculpted from this banality, this street. Ah, how mysteriously the everyday things of life brush by us! On the surface, touched by light, of this complex human life, Time, a hesitant smile, blooms on the lips of the Mystery! How modern all this sounds, yet deep down it is so ancient, so hidden, so different from the meaning that shines out from all of this.

Fernando Pessoa, *The Book of Disquiet*

CONTENTS

ACKNOWLEDGMENTS

I want to thank the members of the Critical Theory Institue at the University of California, Irvine, for providing me the opportunity to give these lectures. I especially want to thank Rey Chow and Jim Fujii for making my stay pleasant and pleasurable in every conceivable way, and Rey in particular for her valuable reading of the original lectures. I also thank Carol Gluck and Bill Haver, whose readings of the lectures have immeasureably enhanced my revision, even if they can't be held responsible for what I have done. I want to record my thanks to Leora Auslander, with whom I first taught a seminar on everyday life at the University of Chicago, and to the students who made our job easy and exciting. My colleagues Louise Young and Hyun Ok Park have generously provided additional critical assessments of the lectures that I have tried to incorporate and for which I am thankful. I want to thank Masao Miyoshi for being around, and Katsuhiko Endo, Ken Kawashima, and Alexandra Monroe, who cheerfully listened to these lectures as they evolved during innumerable discussions. Thanks also to Peter Osborne, whose *Politics of Time* has been invaluable to my own formulations. But my deepest and most enduring debt is to Kristin Ross, who listened to my initial, often incoherent ramblings concerning the substance of the lectures and who read them at every stage of their production with an eye for both intelligibility and clarity that I've not always been able to match. Finally, I want to express my gratitude to Judy Geib and Sabu Rohso for their cover design.

HISTORY'S DISQUIET

INTRODUCTION

The Unavoidable "Actuality" of Everyday Life

The present! It is unfolding before our very eyes. When stepping out the door, one sees there the spectacle in our here. Still more, it is contemporary custom one sees everywhere people go, in the multitude of households themselves, in the diverse places people congregate, in the parks and gardens. . . . And yet this now is, in actuality, moving.
— Kon Wajirō (1929)

"And if the office in the Rua dos Douradores represents Life for me," the Portuguese poet Fernando Pessoa exclaimed through one of his numerous "heteronyms" Bernardo Soares, "the second floor I live in on the same street represents Art. Yes, Art, living on the same street as Life but in a different room; Art which offers relief from life without actually relieving one of living, and which is as monotonous as life itself but in a different way. Yes, for me Rua dos Douradores embraces the meaning of all things, the resolution of all mysteries, except the existence of mysteries themselves which is something beyond resolution."[1] Acutely attuned to everyday modernity in Lisbon in the 1920s, the modernist poet Pessoa marked the distance between the dull, routine monotony of everyday life, filled with minutiae, and the lofty reflections that everydayness inspired, between the past and the now of the present. Aware, moreover, that in modern life no real difference separated the individual life from the streets—both objects with a "common abstract destiny" that signified only "insignificant value" (p. 23), he was nevertheless convinced that this world of "tedium" defined the terrain of experience and determined the conditions for all reflection. Pessoa's "diary" attests to the groundlessness of any transcendental claim to subjectivity that by the early twentieth century, modernists detected everywhere. This recognition accompanied the capitalist modernization that was transforming urban sites into huge industrialized cities housing the everyday lives of the throngs who had left the countryside for work and a different kind of life. In this new scene, only capital itself occupied the position of an agent or subject producing and fixing value in a loop of repetition and reproduction. "I had an immediate sense of the meaninglessness of life," Soares confesses, "seeing, feeling, remembering, forgetting were all one, all mixed up with a slight ache in my elbows, the fragmented murmurings from the street below and the faint sounds of steady work going on in the quiet office" (p. 43).

Pessoa/Soares is describing "life" from a perspective that is "anonymous," "watchful," the experience of merely a "spectator" who has no role in the making of this world and who compares himself to a "fly." "To live, then, is to be other. Even feeling is impossible if one feels today what one felt yesterday, for that is not to feel, it is only to remember today what one felt yesterday, to be the living corpse of yesterday's lost life" (p. 48). Despite living an aspiration that never exceeds "occupying the chair at the table in this cafe, . . . the whole mystery of the world appears before my eyes sculpted from this banality, this street" (p. 49). The Japanese Kon Wajirō and Gonda Yasunosuke were expressing the same sentiment at the same time as they moved through Tokyo's streets, trying to grasp the experience of the now and its meaning for the present. Walter Benjamin was already embarked on his arcades project, which centered on life on the streets of Paris and on its master navigator, the *flaneur*. For Pessoa, everything appeared unbearable, "except life—the office, my house, the streets." But the "totality" supplied relief, by which he meant the consolation offered by the details of everyday life that structured and colonized the lived experience: "a ray of sunlight falling endlessly into the dead office; a street cry that soars up to the window of my room . . . the terrifying objectivity of the world" (pp. 50–51).

The experience was rooted in the present: "I live in the present. I know nothing of the future and no longer have a past" (pp. 60–61), and the present slips into a past that is never worth repeating. But Pessoa seemed to have located the destructive force of modern time in the recognition that nothing lasts (p. 57), and the experience of life itself, "like history," teaches nothing (p. 77).

Before Pessoa laid hold of an experience of the present, James Joyce had mapped the details of a single day lived in the city of Dublin by his protagonist Stephen Daedalus. Marcel Proust had tried to capture the memory of the present of a singular experience that had passed, and countless Japanese and Chinese writers were privileging the details of everydayness in novels concentrating on the individual's experience. It is important to notice that Pessoa was recounting a lived experience in Lisbon, not too different from the so-called I novelists in Japan—who often employed the form of a confessional diary—or even Joyce's Dublin. They all were located on the periphery of the industrial world but still were affected by its transforming processes. We could say the same about the large cities of late-developing countries like Brazil and colonial and semicolonial societies like India and China. This sensitivity to the distinctively modern experience rooted in the present disclosed an awareness of the temporal dimensions of the present and its difference from the pasts that had preceded it. Benjamin named this present the *actuality* of the everyday as it was being lived and experienced in the large industrializing cities. But because the present became the primary and privileged temporality—against which all other moments would be measured—he called for a "Copernican revolution" of memory that would reverse the conventional catalogue and base its procedure not on the fixed reality of the past—as practiced by historians seeking to reproduce it as it actually was and thus establish continuity between the past and the present—but, rather, on the actuality of the present. The now of everydayness would stand in a dialectical relationship to the past that it would construct.

At the heart of Benjamin's project was the elaboration of the philosophical possibility of a "spectral historical experience,"[2] the historiographic rules of the "messianic exception" constituting his understanding of a new materialist history whose realization became compellingly urgent by 1940. What is important to us here is Benjamin's identification of the actuality of the present, to which thinkers in Japan, and everywhere else capitalism was taking root, were appealing as a means of understanding the new they were already living, the now of Tosaka Jun and Kon Wajirō, which differentiated their present from the past. The question that these thinkers were trying to answer was related to the givenness of the historical present and how it showed itself as a present. But what the now of the present offered was little more than a minimal unity empowered to organize the experience of the everyday. That is, to speak of the present already denoted the unification of several givens in a minimal unity of meaning.[3] Moreover, this was a unity in time, marked by a kind of synthesis of apprehension, reproduction, and recognition, what Kantians called the "synthetic unity of experience." In other words, the condition of possibility of an experience of the present—the now—depended on the synthesizing capacity of consciousness. The modern, it was believed, was manifest when the unity formed by this synthesis was constantly dislocated, when consciousness was bombarded with givens that challenged its capacity to assimilate and classify in continuity and sequentiality. At that point, the world—the ever-present now—declared war on consciousness; traumatized it with shock, sensation, and spectacle; and introduced interruption, so that it could no longer dominate its objects and was forced to retreat into the sanctuary of pure memory and a pure past. This is the world that Georg Simmel described in his study of mental and metropolitan life and that Benjamin later divided into "voluntary and involuntary memory." This minimal unity of the present, however precarious, was increasingly seen by thinkers as the actual and unavoidable experience of everydayness that everywhere in the industrializing world—colonized and noncolonized—was identified as distinctively modern.

The chapters of this book, initially presented in 1997 as the Wellek Lectures, are concerned with two interrelated problems: how the category of everydayness was conceptualized as a minimal unity of temporal experience and how it might serve as a historical optic to widen our understanding of the processes of modernity being experienced throughout the world at the same time. This book also examines the encounter between the diverse inflections of the lived experience of everyday life in Euro-America—whose history has always repressed the modernity of the world outside it—and of those regions where it arrived with the exportation of capital and took a number of different forms. The first impulse grows out of my interest in the historical question of modernity and how its experience was conceptualized in the everyday. The other concern derives from my interest in societies outside Euro-America, such as Japan, whose modernity not only has been assimilated to the exemplars of the West but, when it is discussed, also has been seen as either a copy of an original or, worse, an alternative. While such a view may satisfy the need to "provincialize Europe," as Dipesh Chakrabarty has been advising for years, it also strengthens and diversifies our understanding of a process that has always been seen as the achievement of a culturally specific endowment. Above all, this view compels us to confront our present as the starting point for any consideration of the past, when the world outside Euro-America—which in Benjamin's time was still an imprecise shadow beyond historical consciousness, resembling the distant thunder of Satayjit Ray's movie of the same name—can no longer be ignored or repressed.

With the identification of everydayness, there is no longer an outside. That is, I intend to explain how the temporal experience of everyday life ultimately privileged both a contemporary category identifying modernity and a philosophical method—what Tosaka Jun called the "quotidianization of thought"—and a historical category capable of accounting for different social spaces in diverse societies across the spectrum of capitalist modernization. Although the identity of everydayness and the awareness of the primacy of the present signaled at a certain historical moment (the late nineteenth and early twentieth centuries) the formation of a specific experience lived and represented in industrializing cities, it was also a category of historical explanation that enlarged the perspective from which we can explore the contradictions of capitalist modernity. Modernity was generated by a distinct mode of production condensed in the life of the cities and inflected throughout the industrializing world, especially in the semiperiphery and colonial realms of Asia. Even the new socialist state in the Soviet Union tried to conceptualize an everydayness consistent with its own noncapitalist aspirations.

Our concentrating on the conceptualization of the everyday in order to identify a unified experience of modernity does not mean ontologizing the category, as it concerns only how contemporaries organized their lived experience at a certain historical moment and named it and how that moment was historically stored for later interpreters.[4] Despite the failure of the everyday to qualify as an ontological ground, even though many believed it might be so in view of the groundlessness of capitalist modernity, it was still the site of practices that pointed to its open-endedness, incompletion, contradictions, and multiaccentuality, what many recognized as the social space of submerged dreams of the past—a spectral history—and a possibility for the future. Years later, Henri Lefebvre looked at the place of everydayness where alienations were produced from the vast unevenness of lived experience and thus at the site that offers the occasion for critique.

As a historian of societies outside Euro-America, I've always been faced with the task of finding ways to relate this knowledge of an outside local experience to the inside of a larger, more familiar referent capable of explaining comparisons. But it has been difficult to carry out this assignment without destroying the second term by assimilating it to the first, without recuperating the old binary that marks the historical practice of confronting the actuality of societies outside Euro-America. Despite the now-long history of teaching and researching Asian societies, the favored mode is to accommodate the local knowledges so as to make them conform to categories derived from and worked through the study of European and American history. This has meant a rather short itinerary of familiarization which began with the presumption of imitation in response to pronouncements of similarity to progress to a worst case strategy that has resorted to the analogy of the Protestant Ethic to explain Japan's (and China's) work ethic and rapid modernization, an idea still circulating in some putatively serious studies.[5]

This complaint should not, however, be understood as a plea for a "native theory" and concepts, which today is the thoughtless but overdetermined response to a tradition in Asian studies of being marginalized in both the home department (where the area people are always in a numerical minority and have a second-class intellectual status) and the national culture that the specialist represents (in which the outsider's work is assailed for having failed to penetrate the innermost recesses of native sensibility). This institutional practice of marginalization is mirrored especially in the way in which historians have envisioned their discipline and its modes of knowing. Peter Novick's masterful attempt to dignify the high gossip of the American historical profession by narrating its "history" scarcely acknowledges that historical practice is something more than the historiography of the United States, England, and western Europe.[6] In what Novick proposes to be a critique of the profession, he reproduces how it has represented itself and its intellectual concerns as they were figured in the controversy over the question of history's objectivity. Missing, of course, is the world at large, especially its status in the present in which Novick was writing his book, that shadow realm that historians have delegated to the outside as a condition of worrying about whether or not they are scientific and objective. Novick's refusal to stray from professional practice and ideology and willingness to adhere to the constraints of convention positing both an inside and an outside (background noise) echoes H. G. Wells's earlier *History of the World*, which the Japanese native-ethnologist Yanagita Kunio dismissed because it was not about the world as such. Since Wells's history ignored Africa and Asia and much of the rest of the world, it remained nothing more than an Englishman's account of his world, which still tried to masquerade its particularistic conceits as universal truths, that is, the privileged part standing in for the unenvisaged whole.[7]

An even more revealing celebration of the historical view that keeps the outside outside is Richard Evans's well-meaning book *In Defense of History*.[8] Driven by the desire to rework E. H. Carr's earlier (1961) and strangely successful book on history, Evans is concerned with defending the practice of history from its older pieties and its newer, "postmodern" critics. But true to the tradition of maintaining the balance that historians are always advised to keep (as if life itself were balanced), Evans tries to extract something of lasting value from precisely those older historians (mostly

British) who seem to be out of date today (as they were when they were writing, I should add), all the while accommodating some of the newer insights promoted by "postmoderns." We must thank Evans for putting to rest, again, the absurd and now almost comical claims of social historians who in the 1960s and 1970s privileged this kind of historical writing over all others. Inspired by their discovery of the continent of hard, as opposed to soft, data, social historians congratulated themselves for having brought the study of history into the domain of (social) science, announcing confidently the implementation of new quantitative techniques and technology that promised to make their data look even harder and in the very near future would put the historian, as LeRoy Ladurie hoped, into the ranks of computer programmers. (He could have found a more useful career for historians, such as in plumbing or bricklaying.) If it is hard now to see how any of this could have been taken seriously by adults, its promise faded sooner than it takes to install a flush toilet or even to program a computer.

Evans fails to recognize that the project of writing social history depends entirely on the presumption of an unnamed and unarticulated conception of the social, which undoubtedly is derived from a theory of society that only remotely has anything to do with the social formation under examination and about which the historian must necessarily remain silent in order to reconstruct the social past. What I'm driving at is simply that the practice of social history, despite appeals to empirical rigor and hard data, was bonded to a conception of the social that might have been seen as consensual but had no reality. (I am, of course, thinking of the fantasy of Talcott Parsons's social system—the dream of small-town America—which had wide circulation in the 1950s and 1960s until American society was recognized as being far from the consensual totality earlier imagined. There are other, appropriate examples consistent with different national societies.) Evans represses in his devotion to unnamed normativity the vast diversity of the social as it is lived around the globe and in history. This appeal to a normative social is the same tactic used by developmentalists and modernization theorists in the 1950s and 1960s when they tried to incorporate the outside world—then called the *unaligned world*—into the narrative of capitalism.

This misrecognition is not surprising in a book that allows barely two out of two hundred pages for the new histories of the outside, as it were, Asia and Africa—whole continents—while at the same time lavishing unlimited space on a few, individual British historians like Trevelyan, Namier, and Elton that few people outside England read in the past and that nobody today, anywhere, could seriously see as models for historical practice. The asymmetry (imbalance?) of Evans's book may have been partly dictated by the identity and demands of his potential readership. But it also betrays what he believes to be important to history and historiography. We must ask, therefore, what kind of history, and for whom, is being promoted when one affirms historians whose local knowledge of either the seventeenth or the eighteenth century is now made to speak for the whole. In pushing this conceit, Evans is simply reviving an ideology that sees the British present as untroubled and its past as the prefiguration of this happy state. Trevelyan's so-called poetic history has more in common with his aristocratic nostalgia or imperial bards like Tennyson than with later postmodernism. And Namier's blustery dismissal of ideas and ideologies as agents figuring action—as opposed to the aspiration of personal power—always seemed somewhat lame in light of his own ideological passion, on which Evans remains strangely silent. (When I was a student and even years later, the name Namier was invoked as an authority so unimpeachable that its effect was to terrorize and paralyze anybody foolish enough to take ideas and ideology seriously, even though the source of this privilege was never identified.) Ultimately, Evans turns to Leopold von Ranke—one of the canonical figures of history who was not British but German—and to his decision to enlist philology—the "science" of reconstructing dead European languages in order to learn about the prehistorical culture of their speakers—as the model for a rigorous historical practice. But Evans never questions the relationship between this move and a context that would help "provincialize" Ranke and his science.[9]

When Evans turns to his present in order to assess the "postmodernist" critique of the historian's practice, he continues to reinforce the tactic of substituting a local knowledge for a universalistic claim. Throughout his "Defense," he returns to familiar postmodernist theorists like Hayden White, Dominic LaCapra, and the philosopher Frank Ankersmit, along with a few from Great Britain like Patrick Joyce and Keith Jenkins, and the response by historians who have widely condemned this discourse and called attention to the "dangers" posed by the Derridian view that there is nothing outside the text. In the most extreme denunciations, this fear has led to historiographical panic and the warning that "history as we have known it" will soon disappear and "fact and fiction [will] become indistinguishable from one another."[10] Yet what these jeremiads all fail to understand is that the very postmoderns that they are now excoriating are really members of the same historiographical club that they believe is being undermined by the new theoretical perspectives. It is important to note that all these putative "postmoderns" are deeply rooted in the defense of both Western culture and its version of historical consciousness and that this defense, as it is articulated in their texts, could not have been possible without overlooking the cultural specificity of their own location. One of the ironies of this postmodern accent, undetected by either Evans or its critics, is that those who really should know better are as committed to the particular historiographic endowment and its conventions as are those who are now decrying the disappearance of club privileges and rules.

No theorist is more important to this discourse than the historian Hayden White, whose *Metahistory*, along with Edward Said's *Orientalism* and Fredric Jameson's *Political Unconscious*, recalls for us the force of a particular historical conjuncture that would not simply supply new ways to look at history, culture, and politics but, just as important, would reduce the received conventions and approaches to a past not worth retrieving. (A very interesting prehistory of current cultural studies in the United States could be written on the basis of these three seminal texts, which appeared at about the same time.) White's book parallels Said's pathbreaking analysis of knowledge and power in the colonial enterprise, and even though it has not had the impact of *Orientalism* on transforming English studies and revising the canon, it has, I believe, made historians more aware of what they are doing, which an earlier generation could easily and happily overlook by appealing to archival research and the promise of the Rankean dream of objectivity.

Moreover, it is important to notice that Evans fails to contextualize White, whose own tactic was to de-historicize his text in order to give it the appearance of unstudied detachment and scientific rigor and thereby to locate the formation of his discourse in the debate between science and art that prevailed in the 1950s and early 1960s (Vietnam changed that, as well). It is important, too, to recognize that White's book was written at the moment when the end of ideology had already been declared and the neutrality and objectivity of science (and even social science) had been freed from the distortions of false consciousness. In fact, the term *ideology* in the social sciences of the 1950s acquired pejorative associations that it still has not lost. Only art remained captive of the fictions and untruths resembling the unsupported claims of ideology, which meant that history now had to align its disciplinary interests with (social) science if it was to have any credibility in this brave new world that had banished ideology. Behind this controversy over scientific neutrality and ideological distortion was the politics of the cold war and the transmutation of Marxism (communism) into mere ideology and distortion and capitalism and democracy into pluralism and scientific objectivity.

We are indebted to White for trying to resolve this impossible problem for historians, who were already convinced of the scientific basis of their discipline, without thinking too much about it, and thus for shifting history's grounding to art and literature. With one blow, *Metahistory* demolished all the spurious claims of a scientific history—including its deformed offspring, social science history, and the privilege delegated to social history and its conceit promising scientific rigor based on "hard" data (averaging and stockpiling) and the implementation of new technologies not available to Ranke and Burckhardt. What White took with one hand, however, he gave back with another. The argument of *Metahistory* and of most "postmoderns" who have come in its wake and expanded its scope—as Evans notes when citing its critics—was offered as a rigorous scientific exposition whose language and style of structuralist and formalist presentation worked to displace an account that was clearly aimed at showing history's kinship with rhetoric, art, and literature. Moreover, White's effort to simulate the effect of science itself revealed a conception of science then held more often by analytic philosophers than by scientists themselves. His conception of art also relied on Gombrich's understanding of realism and Kenneth Burke's reduction of rhetoric to five master tropes and a linguistic practice that had nothing to do with languages outside Europe.

Armed with this formidable technology, White was able to display how the classic nineteenth-century historical narratives were constructed not on the model of a scientific inquiry but according to the properties of the realist novel. The force and persuasion of these narratives depended less on the context in which they were produced—which is absent in White's account—than on the deployment of formal rhetorical strategies, that is, the emphasis of one master trope over another. Behind this move was Roland Barthes's earlier dismissal of history's fictive appeal to referentiality and Northrop Frye's lifeless new formalism, eschewing history itself, that aimed to equip literary analysis with generic categories to identify the production of literary texts, a veritable new Aristotle. Like Frye, White practiced a rigorous formalism that ironically put the exposition of art within the constraints of scientific form. He thus seemed concerned not with the surface of historical context but with deeply embedded rhetorical structures capable of determining narrative emplotment as one mode or another, like comedy or tragedy.

If White satisfied or, better yet, compensated for the loss of history's claims to being scientific, by making its production appear scientific, he also tried to resolve the nagging problem of bad metaphysics and politics. Depending on the rhetorical strategy and emplotment, the choice would lead to a corresponding politics or ideology. But one was as good as another, signifying the absent contextual force of a prevailing but residual pluralism attending the production of *Metahistory* but never acknowledged and revealing an apoliticality that the Vietnam War had already thrown into question. In a world that confidently announced the end of ideology (to be later followed by the "end of history"), the identification of different ideologies in art—one as good as another—was simply a transformation of a liberal desire for plural interests as the necessary basis for consensus.

If Evans has failed to recognize the relationship between *Metahistory* and the force of a specific context, as most of the critics of this version of "postmodernism," he, like these critics, had trouble explaining why the work was so vehemently discounted. I remember my former colleague, the classical historian Arnaldo Momigliano, literally foam at the mouth when he spoke of this book and its deadly threat to history "as we have known it." Instead, however, White's achievement must be seen as having rescued history as we have known and practiced it. Because he concentrated on the formal categories involved in the formation of historical texts and how the classic narratives were produced, he managed to create a canon for history, just as Said opened the way for a new canon for English studies.

Despite all the charges against him, *Metahistory* actually reaffirmed history's claim to a certain kind of knowledge expressed in a narrative form that still resembles the nineteenth-century realist novel. Even though White was willing to entertain new and even alternative models to composing history, he never explored these possibilities nor, in fact, appealed to available models like those imagined by Walter Benjamin who, as much as Frye or Auerbach, was steeped in a culture of literature but who envisaged an entirely different kind of history that inverted the emphasis on a fixed past and its promise to yield historical knowledge for one that privileged the present and experience as a condition of constructing the past. By seeing history in his revised version of historical materialism as a construction, Benjamin clearly saw the production of history as an act of reading/writing, more aesthetic and ethical than the scientific claims of historicism in the practices of Marxists and non-Marxists alike.

Even more important, White's *Metahistory*, like the writing of most of his "postmodern" followers, supplies the most powerful defense of history's ("as we have known it") identification with a specific historical-cultural endowment produced under the sign of a particular Western modernity, launched by both capitalism and colonialism, whose own condition of possibility was having to maintain that there was no outside. Thus, the practice of reconstructing the past of the West required the narrative of the full subject whose certainty could be secured by insisting on the existence of an excluded and incomplete second term. In this respect, White's *Metahistory* is a far more persuasive defender of the historical practice that Evans wishes to save by his effort to reiterate the tired rules set down by Ranke, as if his "method" and "theory" were not produced by a set of conditions that had everything to do with a specific time and place that we fortunately have outgrown.

But in another way, it is for this reason that we must relate White's *Metahistory* to Said's *Orientalism* precisely because it reaffirms the very cultural endowment and claim to unearthing the historical knowledge that the latter is seeking to undermine by appealing to how knowledge has been used to repress the experience of the excluded second term, the outside to Euro-America's inside. By using a formalist tactic that suppresses context to account for the production of classic narratives, White manages not only to canonize them but also to identify the histories' specific narrative form of emplotment. Yet this is a strange "history" that eschews the contextual reflexivity that robs the narratives of their own historical conditions of production. Although White persuasively argues that different story lines are possible, depending on the steering strategy selected by tropic choice, this plurality of possible plots is far less important than the preservation of a continuist, successive, and progressive movement from a past to a present, which appears to be the real effect of *Metahistory*, even though this intention is never spelled out.

Perhaps it is time to revisit that superior concept of experience that Kant unleashed in spite of himself, as it was perceived first in our century by Benjamin as religion and historical experience that he named as messianic, in which each exception explodes to save a lost justice from the past but which for us is the primacy of the present, the now of our moment and everything that implies. This,

in turn, requires seeking a history for another time, one that rec-
ognizes the immediacy of the present and looks for ways to account
for its "actuality" as a condition of "constructing" a past for it. One
of the principal problems raised by the conventions that both Evans
and White wish to reaffirm, albeit differently, is a belief that relies
on the fixity of the past and its capacity to yield a historical knowledge that can reveal how the present developed from it, even
though the perspective of the present must be detached from the
quest for knowledge. This conception—it probably no longer
needs to be said—is driven by presumptions of continuity and the
conviction, at least in England, that the present constitutes no
problem other than supplying a platform from which the historian
can look back on the past. Distance ensures detachment, if not
ahistoricity itself, as does the application of the methods employed
to extract a knowledge from the archive. It is interesting to see how
the breakup of empire after World War II, the recurring legacies
and living nightmares of decolonization, the cold war, the collapse
of the Berlin Wall, and runaway globalization have so far not
shaken the stability of a historical practice bonded to the fixity of
the past and its promise to reward the faithful historical researcher.
Yet if these events and others force anything, it is precisely the cataclysmic nature of all events and the necessary acknowledgment
of the primacy of the present—the "now of recognizability"—in
any subsequent consideration of a past.

What this cascading of events dramatizes is, above all, the primacy of the present that compels us to look beyond the past of
Euro-America to that repressed outside that has always been there
but whose presence now is more visible than ever before. It can
no longer be indefinitely deferred or displaced in indefensible
metonymic moves that permit historians, say of eighteenth-century
England or indeed any localized and provincial experience, to misrecognize it as the world. Ranke's world was, after all, a small one,
buried in a specific history already inscribed in the production of
his method and historical texts, despite his own claims to universalism. To have figured a "science" devoted to piecing together
shards of dead languages as the model for reconstructing a knowledge of the past affirmed Michel DeCerteau's later observation

that history is concerned with death. It has always puzzled me why historians feel bound to "breathe life" into a dead object that can only result in permanent breathlessness.

Although this presumption of an excluded outside presupposes an epistemological "ground" that gives full subjectivity to those with a certain kind of knowledge, it has authorized a binary differentiation between West and non-West, negativizing the second term and identifying modernity with a specific geopolitical site. But such distinctions, despite their "authorizing" epistemology, are culturally specific concepts that have been used to establish and maintain the fiction of Western unity and to legitimate its "moral" superiority, often projected as universalistic, and can no longer be taken for granted. Any critique, indeed any historical practice, must now be positioned not inside or outside the "West," since the West can no longer be thought of as merely a geographical concept privileged to designate its absent other and to define it in its negativity. Rather, we now must acknowledge a different arrangement that locates practice immanently within the temporality of a modernity embracing new cultural forms that are developing everywhere that demand to be considered as coexistent equivalents with the "West," despite the apparent historical differences among them. In this respect, postcolonial theory, with its aspiration to become an epistemology, has begun this move, despite the aporias it has produced in the process.

A history founded on the "now of recognizability" is not a state, a step in a continuous process, but, rather, a "tableau," a "presentation," a recovery of what was lost, repressed, excluded. Françoise Proust, meditating on Benjamin's conception of historical time, proposed a view that sees history as spectral, inasmuch as such events that seek to restore what had been lost or buried come as specters, apparitions that seek to trouble the present and that are always on the point of arriving, since they have already been expelled from history.[11] In his *Specter of Comparison*, Benedict Anderson alerts us to one of the excluded possibilities lived by societies outside Europe but implicated in its imperial expansion, whose modern forms were thus introduced through the export of capital and colonial de-territorialization. Through a reading of

Jose Rizal's late-nineteenth-century novel, *Noli me tangere*, Anderson is able to perceive how the gardens of Manila were "shadowed . . . by images of their sister gardens in Europe." They can no longer be seen in their immediacy but only from a perspective simultaneously close up and faraway. The novelist names this doubling the "specter of comparison."[12] For Anderson, concerned with resituating the Southeast Asian outside in contemporary analysis, the doubling effect (noted years later in Japan by the philosopher Watsuji Tetsurō, who could not have read Rizal) necessitated thinking simultaneously about Europe and its outside and mandated the establishment of comparative perspectives, in which comparison was always a "haunting." Like all such ghostly arrivals, the appearance of the apparition in the form of comparison works to unsettle the inside—Euro-American civilization—which had enabled the comparison in the first place. In other words, Europe's modernity is already inscribed in its "shadow," which is always in a position to outdo the "original," even though the "original" can never, in revenge, turn on its shadow to undo it.[13]

Beyond Anderson's identification of the ghostly is, I believe, the larger spectrality of societies deeply involved in fashioning a modernity coeval with Euro-America yet whose difference is dramatized by the revenant, the ghosts of what had been past and the premodern culture of reference that had not yet died, returning from a place out of time to haunt and disturb the historical present. This is what Benjamin once recognized as the present conjuring the past. It also means acknowledging that past and present are not necessarily successive but, instead, are simultaneously produced, as Bergson once proposed, just as the here and there of modernity are coeval, even though the latter is often forgotten in the narrative of the former.

What historical practice has excluded in its desire to narrativize a cultural aspiration is the relationship between itself and the modernities of the world outside it that share both the same temporality and a transformative process driven by the agency of the same mode of production. This historical specter entails seeing history not from the presumption of a fixed past capable of yielding a historical knowledge, which is the past of Europe's present empowerment.In modern times, the fixity of the national past has dominated historical practice. Rather, it seems important to start with the now of the present and invite the configuration of a relationship to a past in such a way as to reveal the possibility of another kind of narrative based on the "exceptional" structured from the present's desire. Here, there is no appeal to a distancing and abstracting "detachment" at the same time the historian is embracing an impossible empathic identification, as if the observer and observed were one. What has been absent in the practice of history devoted to reconstructing the past of a present is the present, what is given as the historical present and how it shows itself. As I've suggested, our present—indeed, any present—can be nothing more than a minimal unity that I call the *everyday* that has organized the experience of modernity. Consisting of the primacy of the now, this minimal experience of unity is always unsettled by the violence of events that the receiving consciousness disaggregates not as memory as such but as trace, not as a figured image but as "cinders," remains left by a devastating trauma. These remains roam about like the dead (or perhaps the undead)—what Benjamin once called "involuntary memory"—who wait for their hour to return among the living and upset their present, like specters waiting to avenge themselves if the present fails to remember them.

What distinguishes modernity is consciousness of time and how it relates its present to both past and present. If all events are catastrophic, constantly destroying the new landscape, it will not be time that successively carries away each now, each present. Rather, each present is empty, vacated of meaning at the moment it arrives.[14] Hence the ruin is not an effect of time, the delimitation of things under the effect of time's passing and "polishing." The ruined historical landscape is in the same state as the modernity of things. All production immediately falls into ruin, thereafter to be set in stone without revealing what it had once signified, since the inscriptions are illegible or written in dead languages. All events necessarily bear a trace, a mark, an inscription, and hence an indication that it has passed into the past. This is not to say that all events produce an official document, a sudden commemoration, or even a collective memory. Conversely, all collective remembrance, all "voluntary memory," is made for protecting the self from shock, those projectilelike events regularly discharged by modernity. By incorporating the events into history, it is the purpose of tradition to level out and smooth the rugged edges, ease the sudden starts, and naturalize the historical productions. Beneath the historical present, however, lie the specters, the phantoms, waiting to reappear and upset it.

Since for historians the date is the proper name of an event, connoting its temporality, notifying, signifying, and recalling that something had once occurred, knowing it meant filling it out, placing it in a visible order with a "face." But dating in this manner corresponded to a temporal order. In order for temporality to become legible, what Benjamin in "Central Park" referred to as giving dates a "physiognomy" so that they could be given a visible order, required turning to its corollary in space, which meant knowing the places that housed history's dates and events.[15] In modernity, during the epoch of industrialization and the establishment of mass society, the places of history are the cities, the expanding industrial sites, and their experiences are the everyday. It is thus the cities, not anymore the countryside in general, that make up the contemporary scene, the now of the present. This scene is the stage that both figures the experience of the everyday and provides the space on which it is enacted, and it is vastly different from the immemorial daily life lived in the countryside, the villages, and even those premodern cities surrounded by a rural political economy. The modernity of everydayness is the streets, the buildings, the new institutions and constant movement, the ceaseless interrelationship between public and private that register large and small events alike. It is henceforth in the cities that modern technologies are installed, producing consumer commodities in times of peace and instruments of destruction in times of war. Everydayness is precisely the space of immanence that dissolves the received binary between inside and outside and within which we must locate historical practice. And it is in the cities that the everyday writes its own history.

In the following chapters I hope to show how the streets, buildings, and shops have constantly supplied the means to write themselves and how the signs they offered were first configured by thinkers and writers into a conceptualization of everydayness, in Europe and its outside, but notably in the case of Japan. Put differently, I would like to propose not a social history of a historical conjuncture as such or a reconstruction of a moment in the past but, rather, a cultural history of memory (after François Dosse's program for a social history of memory) that is concerned less with the event structure and its telling than it is with the traces supplied by those who could recall a lived experience at the moment it was occurring.[16] If this comes close to what we used to call intellectual history, it differs significantly in its rejection of the model of reconstruction, based on the present's relationship to a fixed past and its capacity to yield a historical knowledge. "With the first movement," Dosse writes, identifying the necessary double structure of historical practice,

> which ensures primacy with regard to critique, at the putting of distance, to objectification and to demythologization, follows a second, complementary moment, without which history would be pure exoticism, that of recollection of the sense of meaning, which aims at appropriating diverse sedimentations of meaning bequeathed by preceding generations, the possible but not established [experiences] that litter the past with defeats, and of the silence of history.[17]

This entails a perspective that privileges the present and its necessity to constitute the past and the willingness to abandon a "scientific" model based on a theory of mechanical causality that presupposes identifying the cause of an effect in the immediate anteriority on the temporal chain.[18]

The signs produced by the everydayness of the city had to be understood as emblems of a particular lived experience of the present and its historical difference, as an "afterimage," a trace of what once had been actualized and that the present actualized anew in a different configuration. What proved to be emblematic were the details, the objects, important or not, that filled the space and colonized everyday life. If Siegfried Kracauer and Benjamin, or even the Soviet constructivist Boris Arbatov, enshrined the place and the experience of things, Japanese contemporaries living a coeval modernity, like Kon Wajirō, made the study of things into an object of research, what he called "modernology," and Tosaka Jun called for the quotidianization of philosophy that could rethink the relationship of material space—the city—to time. What thinkers recognized in modern everyday life was the experience of classes, notably that of the newly emerged industrial worker, but, just as important, the details and objects that formed the conditions of lived experience. In this regard, the city especially offered the occasion for contemplating and recounting in its myriad signs "forgotten yet unforgettable meanings," waiting there like mute allegories to be "reawakened."[19]

What everydayness signified for all who lived its reality and read the history it wrote was the way the now actualized the past that lay waiting in the present, not the having been but the "forgotten yet unforgettable." As I have conceived it, everydayness is a form of disquiet, a moment suspended; it is a new present, a "historic situation" that violently interrupted tradition and suspended the line and movement of the past. Yet lining the routines and rhythms of everyday life, Henri Lefebvre once observed, is another existence that "has a secret life and a richness of its own."[20] In this way, the now of everydayness, as Tosaka argued, holds its evidence and its force of actuality in its capacity to actualize the promises not kept in the present and to reveal the possibilities for critique and renewal that its negativity has concealed. The act of actualization requires a different approach. Instead of treating what has been seen in a historical manner, it is necessary to do so in a political mode with political categories, that is, "authentic historical images" that are not simply archaic, which belong to a more conventional practice, or even one closer to Heidegger's program of "historicality." Appealing to a "political mode" means rooting perspective in the view of the actual. In this sense, history is not mere memory, the remembrance of the way things were, the detached view promising to show what "actually happened," conservation, or even the archive. The tendency still to identify history with memory is nothing more than the sign of a conservative epoch dreaming only of the status quo, desiring no more than what has already arrived. If the term has any sense, history thus envisioned must always be a history of the present, which means a politically driven history, but only if the interventions force critical moments of time and enable the realization of promises that are not kept but that are still transmitted and recovered by tradition. Through the action of the actual present, time is destroyed and constructed. "It must," according to Proust, "be reread or more precisely *read*, and this is the task of critique."[21]

Chapter 1 of this book situates the study of an Asian society—Japan—in the institutional framework of area studies as they were developed after World War II. It shows how area studies were complicit in keeping the outside on the outside. I also try to imagine how everydayness might more effectively serve as a candidate for a cultural studies capable of dissolving the presumptions of a visible inside and repressed outside. Chapter 2 explains how the immanence of everydayness was conceptualized into a minimal unity by a number of thinkers in the early twentieth century as a category for analysis. Chapter 3 examines its doubling in Japan that is occurring at the same moment, even though it is conjugated differently. But it is precisely in this doubling that the "shadow" performed by Japan returns as the revenant to the "original" to haunt the modernities that had both supplied the model Japan employed in its own transformation and excluded its possibility by assigning it to either colonialism or some form of imitation and the status of a copy. In this way, the inflection of Euro-America's modernity turned back to become a critique of it. In other words, we have in this instance two sets of doubling: the return of the ghosts of a not yet completed past to disturb the present of the modern everyday that Japanese were experiencing and the revenant from the outside that returns to unsettle Euro-America's own modernity in the form of a critique that demands recognition and release from its indeterminate state of impossibility, living as the undead.[22] Although I have concentrated on Japan as an example of how the repressed outside of Euro-America underwent the passage of capitalist modernization to produce its own experience of everydayness that would serve as both specter to Europe's own claims and the space revisited by its own revenant, I am persuaded that any society being transformed by modernity would serve as well . With Japan, exceptionalizing the uniqueness of achievement happened to be a condition of the shock of modernity.

1. TRACKING THE DINOSAUR

Area Studies in a Time of "Globalism"

You've established a wonderful thing here with Hitler. . . . Nobody on the faculty of any college or university in this part of the country can so much as utter the word Hitler without a nod in your direction, literally or metaphorically. This is the center, the unquestioned source. . . . It must be deeply satisfying for you. The college is internationally known as a result of Hitler studies. It has an identity, a sense of achievement. You've evolved an entire system around this figure, a structure with countless substructures and interrelated fields of study, a history within a history. I marvel at the effort. It was masterful, shrewd and stunningly preemptive. It's what I want to do with Elvis.
—Don DeLillo, White Noise

It has been one of the enduring ironies of the study of Asia that Asia itself, as an object, simply doesn't exist. While geographers and mapmakers once confidently named a sector on maps, noting even its coordinates as if in fact it existed, this enmapped place has never been more than a simulacrum of a substanceless something. It refers only to itself in the expectation that something out there will eventually correspond to it or be made to align with it. The cartographers' art has been produced by an age-old fantasy and then reinforced by requirements of World War II. Nonetheless we have in this country professional organizations devoted to the study of this simulacrum, and educational institutions pledged to disseminating knowledge of it, even as the object vanishes before our eyes once we seek to apprehend it. I always felt that a professional organization like the Association of Asian Studies periodically brought specialists together in order to reaffirm the existence of what clearly is a phantom. So confident in its existence, this professional body years ago decided to change its name from the Far Eastern Association to the Association of Asian Studies in order to stake out an even larger territory, however phantasmagoric. But these names are as lifeless as the social science—geography—that once declared their reality and named its presence. What seems so important is the way the association tries to sustain the fictional phantom even as its mode of organizing and operating disperses Asia as a coherent figure of knowledge. Anybody familiar with the workings of this association or who has had a glimpse of its journal or the programs of the annual meetings will immediately realize that if Asia is absent, smaller geographic units such as Southeast Asia, East Asia, and South Asia are everywhere represented. A closer look will show that even these satellite units have shrunk into smaller categories of the nation-state.

Although the association's committees are divided along area lines, its membership and officers serve as metonyms—stand-ins—because they are, at bottom, not specialists of Northeast Asia, South Asia, or Inner Asia but of nation-states. In every year's abstract there is a section near the back of the volume devoted to "interarea," yoked to the categories of library and teaching, marking its location of "in betweenness" and suggesting both expedience and afterthought. All this signifies the recognition that an association committed to the study of Asia is not an "interarea" when in fact its true vocation would be to extract or produce knowledge that could be only interarea. Nobody ever questions the directional tyranny that names as East the place we go to study. East is, rather, where one ends up when starting from the geographical West, which implies that movement can proceed in only one direction. But this inversion of the earlier Hegelian itinerary of freedom's unfolding as it moves slowly from east to west confirms its intellectual trajectory favoring the place of the West which, because of its full and completed development, can view the East from this privileged site. But where do we really start from, where is the place of enunciation?

When we try to account for how an association devoted to Asia determines the principles on which panels are "selected for its annual meeting," we learn that apart from the exercise of political interest—invariably denied—no other criteria seem to inform the breakdown besides the traditional disciplines and national societies.

Panels belong to either a discipline and/or a national society around which papers have been organized. A few years ago, a proposal for a two-part panel dedicated for the first time to examining area studies was reduced to one part by the selection committee, and its placement suggested that the association was indifferent, if not outrightly hostile, to self-reflection. In 1996, a president's round table was scheduled to discuss the status of area studies in a profession that has never shown the slightest interest in its enabling epistemology and the structure of organization it has authorized. But multipart panels still continue to be formed to examine arcane subjects like medicine in Tokugawa Japan as if such a subject, and others even more remote and specialized, were so compelling that students were actually waiting in line to get the latest word. I always suspected that this arrogance could be traced to the association's desire to appear "unpolitical" and functioned to repress its political origin, which plainly was generated by political considerations after World War II. While this newly articulated, self-reflexive interest in the status of area studies stems from the widely acknowledged bankruptcy of the model, it was undoubtedly prompted by the Ford Foundation's recent program to fund the effort to rethink area studies in fifty colleges and universities.

Once the organization of area knowledge was fixed, soon after World War II, all that remained were periodic adjustments to the changing political realities throughout the world and discussion of how the structures it sanctioned could be sustained. This anxiety was expressed in the obsessive search for money here and abroad, which has become the principal preoccupation of area studies in the established universities and colleges of the United States and probably the United Kingdom.

The reluctance to cross the administrative/geopolitical and disciplinary grids that partition knowledge means only that the informing principles of a dominant tradition in the social sciences and the humanities continue to authorize the still axiomatic duality between an essentialized, totalized, but completed Western self and an equally essentialized, totalized but incomplete East. Yet we can see that this refusal to tamper with epistemological and organizational categories is at the heart of the Asia profession and its institutionalization into the model of area studies. Fifty years after the war, we are still organizing knowledge as if—in the case of Japan, China, and the former Soviet Union—we are confronted by an implacable enemy and thus driven by the desire to know it in order to destroy it or learn how to sleep with it. While nobody would deny that this tireless industry has produced mountains of empirical data on the peoples of these societies, this accomplishment has kept these areas from being assimilated into new theories of knowledge and categorizations that promise to end their isolation. The paradox has been that even while we go from a place marked as the West to study the East, we—as Westerners—conspire to keep the two sectors of the globe from encountering each other, shadowing the Hegelian conceit that once spirit left its abode in the East to reveal itself fully in the West, nothing more needed to be said about that part of the world and history, which would remain incomplete until it remade itself in the image of its "other," the self. Like the exotics of an earlier generation, we still seek to penetrate the East and unravel its mysteries, despite knowing that there are none, but we never bring the East back to the world we started from, thus making sure that the East remains the East. In doing so, we preserve the "mysteries" and become its custodians. Perhaps like the intrepid Victor Segelan, we discover there is no there, no mysteries to behold or to report back, and so we have no choice but to preserve the aura by resorting to separation and isolation.

This is, in fact, an apt description of area studies practiced in universities and colleges as their proponents have sought to maintain them in a world increasingly more global and culturally borderless than when they were introduced into the academic procession. What started out as a convenient way to get courses and languages of distantly foreign countries into college and university curricula after the war became, in time, an enormous organization, resembling more a huge holding company with a tight grip on its subsidiaries, monopolizing its product—knowledge of a specific area—and thus controlling its distribution and consumption. Like those temporary dwellings hastily assembled during World War II, presumably to be replaced by something more permanent in the near future, area studies have outlived their original purpose and temporary function to become an entrenched structure that has maintained the separation of knowledge of an area from being integrated into a general pedagogy and curriculum, as it was supposed to. As a result, they have become like fossils entrapped in amber, and today, they still behave more like a dinosaur whose immense body incessantly demands food but whose small head is no longer adequate to control its movements.

Even though the structures representing area studies in colleges and universities are both well staffed and well financed these days, intellectually they are nothing more than worn-out hovels, like the corrugated Quonset huts left on American campuses by the military that served as temporary classrooms and offices well into the 1960s. Even after those structures were eventually dismantled, we still have area studies to remind us of another and a different world, dinosaurs in an intellectual Jurassic Park, where creatures with large bodies and small brains are on display.

The development of area studies programs after World War II grew out of a wartime necessity. Readers of Ruth Benedict's *The Chrysanthemum and the Sword* will recall her acknowledgment that the book was commissioned by the Office of War Information and that its purpose was to better understand the enemy we were fighting. [1] Likewise, the systematic formation of area studies in the major universities was a massive attempt to relocate the enemy in the new configuration of the cold war. This relocation was made possible by large infusions of money from private corporations, scholarly organizations like the Social Science Research Council (SSRC)—"brokering" (pimping might be a more apt description of its role) for both government and private funders—and businesses. This intervention was not simply limited to American universities. The Rockefeller Foundation poured a lot of money into reorganizing the social sciences in France to give the French a new and more scientific social science capable of combating the claims of Marxism. During the Vietnam War, the Ford Foundation tried to support Southeast Asian studies at Kyoto University and for years has been active in both India and Indonesia. In fact, the cold war easily replaced the wartime necessity of learning the enemies' languages and customs by establishing a closer link between the task of identifying the foe and gathering knowledge — intelligence — about it.

As a field of inquiry finding its own place at the end of the academic procession in colleges and universities, area studies was a response to the wartime discovery of the paucity of reliable information concerning most of the world outside Europe. In the immediate postwar period, the recognition of this deficiency was made more compelling by the military, political, and economic expansion of the United States in its effort to reconfigure the world. Underscoring this new urgency and giving it force were a number of reports issued by official and semiofficial commissions immediately after the war that called for the rapid installation of multidisciplinary programs, composed of specialists in various disciplines to train area specialists and provide policymaking and business strategies with informed, socialized knowledge of specific areas. This mode of reporting has characterized the development of area studies and has — in the case of Japan where responsibility has passed from the SSRC to the Japan Foundation and the Japanese Ministry of Education — become a form of surveillance and even censorship, about which I shall say more later.

The University of Michigan geographer Robert B. Hall headed the SSRC's Committee on World Area Research which emphasized the need for an "integrated" approach and the primacy of contemporaneity, suggesting that an interest in historical cultures was no longer useful to government and business.[2] Hall, it should be recalled, had been the president of the Association of Asian Studies and also one of its founders, who subsequently established the Center for Japanese Studies at the University of Michigan and ended his career as the director of the Asia Foundation's office in Tokyo, which sponsored clandestine activities in East Asia. The Commission on the Implications of Armed Services Programs, sponsored by the American Council of Learned Societies (ACLS), recommended the establishment of area specialists, recruited from graduates of the service language schools, to supply reliable knowledge on specific areas. Corporate interests were early reflected in the active involvement of private foundations, like Rockefeller's inau-

gural gifts to Yale to establish Far Eastern and Russian studies and
the University of Washington's program in Far East studies and
Columbia University's Russian Institute. The Carnegie Corpora-
tion gave Harvard $740,000 to establish its Russian Research Cen-
ter in 1947 and, later, almost as much to the University of Michigan
for Japanese studies. Between 1953 and 1966, the principal private
funder for area studies was the Ford Foundation, which awarded
more than $270 million to thirty-four universities and also financed
projects like Princeton University's "Modernization of Societies"
and the University of Chicago's "New Nations Project" in the 1960s.
Even after the government took over this responsibility with the passage of the National Defense Education Act in 1956, private foundations continued to underwrite established area studies programs
and, in time, were joined by overseas foundations associated with
foreign governments and private organizations.

I should point out that the establishment of area studies
programs promised to "transcend" disciplinary boundaries—
partitioned knowledge—to provide holistic and integrated
accounts of different societies. But because of the relentless kinship that area studies formed with policymaking, serving national
interests and, according to Ravi Arvand Palat, "contract research,"
they could never free themselves from the pursuit of a knowledge
bonded to its original purpose. In a 1970 report on Japanese Studies for the SSRC, John W. Hall, formerly of Yale University,
described Japanese area studies programs and its personnel as a
national resource.[3] During the Vietnam War, Professor John K.
Fairbank of Harvard University, literally the last emperor of Chinese studies in the United States, reiterated the instrumentalist
theme that the war dramatized how little Americans knew about
Asia and that it was important to both government and private business to support Asian (Chinese) area studies. But this was an
already exhausted echo of the plea for area studies to meet the
challenges of the cold war in the years immediately after 1945. Yet
it was precisely this division of intellectual labor marking area studies—their service to the state and business and even to foreign governments—that discouraged the discussion of an integrated knowl-

edge of the area and instead encouraged its continued partitioning and fragmenting. The importance of Hall's study, a model for subsequent surveys, is that it prefigured all future efforts to transfer scholarly and pedagogical considerations to the problem of funding area studies programs.

Area studies during the cold war managed to reduce the region under study to the category of national society, as if China, Japan, or Korea could serve as a stand-in for East Asia, or Mexico and Brazil for Latin America, or Bengal for South Asia. With few momentary exceptions like the old New Nations Program at the University of Chicago, funding agencies like the SSRC and ACLS and university teaching and research programs have been organized along the lines of national societies throughout the cold war and after. But even the New Nations project employed the model of the nation as an emergent unit. Despite the SSRC's recent warning that the time has come to "become conscious" of how the organization of international scholarship is patterned on past public and foreign policy and funder priorities, its committees still follow the national model. Even though a recent report announced a shift from country toward "a range of themes," the SSRC has delegated the task of envisaging new models for international scholarship to the very national committees that are supposedly being phased out. This hypocrisy is compounded by the fact that the SSRC has periodically called for reform and revisions only when "funders' priorities" change and money for area studies stops flowing into its coffers.[4] Like Hegel's owl, it is always too late.

In the immediate postwar era, calls for the establishment of new area studies programs revealed the kind of knowledge desired. William Fenton's "Area Studies in American Universities" of 1947 observed that the very methodology of integrated studies was a new challenge. "In taking a functional view of contemporary civilizations," he wrote, "it jeopardizes the strong position which the historical method holds in academic thinking." The new functional approach concentrates on the present situation with its "latent historicity, in place of long developmental curricula running from Aristotle to modern times." And "it calls on the method of the cultural historian to develop the major themes in the civilization, delving deep enough into the past only to make the present under-standable."[5] In time, this became an invitation to abandon history altogether, as functionalist social science explicitly demanded in the 1950s and 1960s. Although the older social science, focus-ing on the interaction of culture and the formation of person-ality—exemplified at war's end by Benedict and Francis Hsu—cooperated with this recommendation to eliminate the long duration of history, or even historical specificity, it could not ade-quately account for explaining the proccesses of change and devel-opment considered so vital to cold war policy strategies designed to win the hearts and minds of the free and unaligned world. Indeed, it had no way to provide for a society's capacity to change and thus risked making modern social groups appear identical with their stone-age predecessors.

Because of this epistemological weakness, a different kind of social science, capable of explaining development and change, was needed, especially one that could offer an alternative to Marxian conflict models and the conception of revolutionary change. It was provided by structural functionalism, which rearticulated the social Darwinist conception of evolutionary adaptation and development and was reconfigured into an export model of growth called *mod-ernization* and *convergence theory*. What was eventually offered as both a representation of and a prescription for development was an evolutionary model of growth, as opposed to a revolutionary one, which, if followed, would lead to the peaceful development of capitalism and, presumably, democracy in the nonaligned world. Even today, the *New York Times* regularly reports, as it did on Sunday, March 9, 1997, quoting President Clinton's former economic adviser Laura D'Andrea Tyson, that American policy is based on, and is thus served by, the conviction that the growth of capitalism and presumably a middle class in China will lead to a "stable evolution toward a more open, more democratic, more market-oriented system based on the rule of law."

Claiming a normative status but appearing more as an ideal-ization scarcely reflecting any recognizable American society on which it was supposed to be based, this theory was inspired by Tal-cott Parsons's theoretical patternings and Marion Levy's unusable applications that often recalled a Rube Goldberg drawing rather than an analysis of a specific social system. Its theory of knowledge rested on a number of ideal typical traits: societies as coherently organized systems whose subsystems were interdependent and on historical development (divided into modern and traditional) that determined social subsystems (in this scheme, modernity meant rational, scientific, secular, and Western; historically, modernization was evolutionary). Last, traditional societies, owing to the success of modernization, would undergo adaptive upgrading.[6] Modernization theory shared with Marxism and, later, postcolonial discourse its refusal to recognize modernity as a specific cultural form and a consciousness of lived historical time that differed according to the various social forces and practices that depended as much on the experience of place as they did on time.

In the scholarly world of the 1950s, 1960s, and early 1970s, this strategy generally dominated research agendas related to area studies, as they still do in policy considerations, even though the cold war has officially ended. During this time, marked by the Vietnam War, its most spectacular success was supplied by the example of Japan and the singularity of the national model. Modernization theory seemed to be able to validate the category of national society more easily than could a heterogeneous area like East Asia and show how a country like Japan could successfully reproduce the necessary patterns when others, like India and Turkey, could not. It was for this reason that Japanese political arrangements have consistently been represented as a democratic stand-in for capitalist development when, in fact, they are driven by a single party devoted to managed capitalism rather than the "free play" of the market. Japan has had to enact a narrative free from conflict and contradiction, in which traditional values could adapt to new exigencies and perform as rational agents. It is important to notice that the category of the nation is made to stand in for the area or region and that the efforts to present a coherent East Asia appeal to the binding power of a religion or an ethic as they fuse comfortably with capitalism (usually referred to as "Asian values"), which stretches the imagination as much as it insults the intelligence. The force of national or ethnic metonyms seem also to have migrated to postcolonial studies, in which Bengal is made to represent the subcontinent.

One effect of modernization theory was to transmute a prescriptive into a descriptive, the rational into the real, an ought into a what is, as the former ambassador to Japan, Edwin O. Reischauer, put it in numerous speeches to Japanese audiences during his tenure in the early 1960s.[7] One consequence of this tactic for the study of societies like Japan has been to discourage the importation of newer theoretical approaches (sensitive to knowledge/power, cognizant of colonizing experiences, and the like) in order to defend the representation of what has been naturalized as a sign of empirical research. According to modernization theory, Japan has thus become a walled enclave resisting newer theoretical approaches. In fact, Japan's "success" as a modernizer exceeded the expectations of its formulators to the extent that Japan, as Reischauer early and ceaselessly reminded audiences, is really not like other Asian countries but is closer to the advanced Western societies it has emulated. For this reason, the Japan field has never shown much inclination to "validate," theoretically or methodologically, the field,[8] which itself never questions the conceptual status of a "field" called "Japan" but, rather, continues to serve a national interest, first that of the United States and then of Japan. Organizations like the SSRC, especially, and the Japan Foundation, presumably devoted to "cutting edge" methodology, have made sure that the national committee structure directing their respective activities (distributing funds and controlling research) serve as the sole custodians of and vigilant guard dogs against particularly the kinds of theoretical and methodological innovations they purport to promote. Instead of encouraging greater integration of differing knowledges and intellectual agendas, they have only partitioned and dispersed them, supported by the national committee structure with its received views of region. The jealously guarded defense of a particular view of an area, say Japan, is matched by the reproduction of institutional and organizational structures (like the composition of committees distributing funds for fellowships and research) that reinforce claims of "normativity." It is here that the negative desire for theory at the heart of area studies is defined and repressed.

If it is hard to take seriously the SSRC's recent declarations that the area studies model is no longer operable, it is even more difficult to believe a plan that places responsibility for implementing the needed changes in the very committees that created the problem. The worst consequence of this repetition is the aggressive dismissal of new theoretical and methodological approaches that might disturb the representation of Japan as signified and its sponsored study by organizations like the SSRC, the Japan Foundation, and that durable instrument of the Japanese Ministry of Education, the Center for the Study of Japanese Culture in Kyoto. What I am suggesting is that these and other entrenched agencies are committed to sustain a particular (and uncritical) conception of Japan and how it should be studied and taught. This conception is linked to institutional structures and sources of funding. More often than not, the same people who represent the interests of large programs have replicated that venerable Japanese practice of "lifetime job security" and sit for long durations on the various national and binational committees distributing money. At one time, this feudal arrangement made no effort to disguise its operations and simply brought the same faces to the same windows.

Apart from the large institutional and financial inducements that encourage the study of the area from the optic of the nation, the nation as a category often determines how people will study it. Many who rushed to a study for personal reasons (missionary connection, service experience, delayed and infantile exoticisms) usually masked such emotional attachments with appeals to empirical and "scientific" authority. The early generation of Americans who raced to study Japan after the war, for example, were committed to showing how the nation's history disclosed the rule of reason (which apparently had been on holiday a few years earlier) and how closely the modernizing experience resembled the example of the United States. (In this project, scholars were assisted by the experience of the U.S. military occupation, which saw Japan as a social laboratory for social democracy and an opportunity for fine tooling and thus improving on the American experience by removing its defects.) This fantasy was projected by the work of modernization studies, sponsored by the Ford Foundation, which effectively worked to transform former foe into friend and trading partner.

Yet this project also disguised or misrecognized the semi-colonial status of Japan (it had already forgotten about Japan's fascism and its recent history as a colonizer) after the U.S. occupation ended. The consequences of this transformation were revealed in subsequent teaching and research showing that Japan most nearly replicated the development of the capitalist and democratic West, despite its brief affair with fascism. When relations between the two partners began to fall apart over trade in the 1970s, critics of this rosy representation were denounced as Japan bashers, usually by professional Japanologists who unwittingly betrayed their own carefully hidden stakes in maintaining an "upbeat" version by trying now to preserve what experience had already repudiated.

China studies seemed to be dominated by the paradigm of challenge and response (actually an old Toynbeean idea recycled by Fairbank and his personal army of students) that saw China responding to the West and failing, owing to retrograde institutions and intellectual traditions, often described negatively as the "nondevelopment of science" and the "nondevelopment of capitalism," paralleling the non-Western outside of Euro-America. Early interpreters of South Asia (in what used to be called "empire studies") easily and enthusiastically overlooked colonialism and attributed all of India's postcolonial problems as a fledgling democracy to the dead hand of religion and overpopulation, as if the subcontinent had never been colonized. With South Asia, the approach to the region still seemed to be clouded by Hegel's dim assessment of the negativity of India life.

If the link between professional Japanologists and the field of study appears more prominent and overdetermined than in other area studies, it is, I believe, because of the overwhelming production of native knowledge and thus self-consciousness that has marked Japan's own modernity. But this enhancement of native knowledge is also a kind of an occupational handicap that dogs the study of Asia especially and other parts of the world outside

Euro-America. Area interest is powered by a mix of exoticisms, however displaced, and a desire for nearness, closing the distance between there and here and the promise of difference. During my first trip to Japan, I met all kinds of Americans fulfilling their exotic and erotic fantasies for reidentification, ranging from obsessive *kanji sharks*, as they were called (the craze to learn as many Chinese ideographs as the mind was capable of retaining, especially those with several strokes) to those who wore baskets on their head, carried rice bowls, and pretended they were itinerant Buddhist pilgrims. We might call this hermeneutic strategy the *Pierre Loti effect*, which is easily recognized as a way of making contact with otherness through a reliance on costume and performance. Since then, only the objects promising identification have changed. (The latest example is the male American who, after a brief stay in Japan, has written a novel from the viewpoint of a geisha, which is about to made into a movie by Spielberg!) With China, there was the "helping hand," the vanished missionary vocation, and the seeming helplessness of the Chinese people in the face of Japan's aggression. Later, for a moment, it was the romance of revolution. With Japan, there is, of course, the legacy of the American occupation and the romanticization of this partnership to rebuild a free and prosperous Japan. Many postwar Japan specialists had come from either missionary families or service language schools; others experienced the occupation as a colonial opportunity. This gave Japan a special status, a uniqueness that was built into programs that always required trainees to go to Japan to do their fieldwork.

When I was a graduate student studying history, I was puzzled by the way Japan was presented as a field where one went to do fieldwork, even if one's purpose was archival rather than ethnographic. People were always off to the field or just returning from it. Even so, they were not as clothes conscious as today's news correspondants who always seem to be outfitted by Banana Republic when on assignment in the "field." But by the same measure, I knew that France, Italy, and England were countries where people went for study and research, whereas Japan, Asia, and Africa were simply fields, places that required observation, recording, and, in some instances, intervention. Perhaps this sense of the field revealed the deeper relationship of these regions to a colonial unconscious, which still approached them as spaces occupied by "natives" who needed to be observed and thus represented. This differentiation between field and country suggested both distance, physical and figural, and the existence of different temporalities marking the boundary between modern and premodern. As students, we were encouraged to spend time in the field to observe societies that belonged to a different temporality, even though we all inhabited the time of the present. It was a Western present, however, established according to "modern" timekeeping. Its most important effect was to classify the field as inside and native and us as visitors from the outside and nonnative seeking entry in order to penetrate and thus grasp the secrets of native knowledge, which would always be beyond reach.

The conceit of transforming a place into a "field" was a custom long practiced by anthropologists and ethnographers, who saw the field as a code for the laboratory; now it became a commonplace among historians, political scientists, sociologists, and students of literature. Persuaded to view Japan or China (which at the time was closed to Americans, who had to use surrogates like Taiwan and Hong Kong), India, and Southeast Asia as ethnographic scenes, students were required to take intensive language courses and to experience living among the natives. These two conditions were considered—and still are—as more than adequate substitutes or replacements for theory and methodology; in fact, they were seen as functional analogues of both. Moreover, trainees in Japanese studies since the end of the war have regularly acquired wives who could double as native informants and stand in for field experience during their time away from the "field." If this often constituted a kind of rite of passage, it also sealed an identity with Japan that further foreclosed the possibility of critique. I should also say that this relationship was usually one way, with men acquiring Japanese wives.

This relationship revealed a deeply embedded hermeneutic that had always promised to promote empathic immediacy and identification as the most appropriate and authentic mode of studying Japan and, I suspect, Asia. It is for this reason that so much emphasis was placed on translation, which apparently produced access to a transparent reality. This epistemological assumption betrays its own racist conceit in the belief that only natives are able to stand in the place of the native. (I remember being reminded by Japanese scholars that I would never truly understand either their language or their culture, which were seen as interchangeable. Although they were probably right for the wrong reasons, the charge presupposed the totally indefensible, if not impossible, acquisition of perfect-transparent knowledge as the only condition for gaining access to the real!) It is important to remember, too, that this conception of a hermeneutic, based on the primacy of and experience in the field ("field time," we should call it) and the "desire" for native or near-native language proficiency and identification, has marked both the way regions are studied and the conditions that inhibit the practice of theory in constructing research and intellectual agendas, which are dismissed out of hand and even denounced in "field" journals like the *Journal of Japanese Studies, Harvard Journal of Asiatic Studies*, and *Monumenta Nipponica*.

Terrorist denunciation has become one of the main vocations of such field journals today, which notoriously act solely as custodians of what can only be described as the authenticity of native knowledge and native concepts, as if native experience anywhere, much less Japan, remained immune from the threat of modernity's promise to eliminate all received cultures of reference. Indeed, the very persistence of field journals devoted to the singularity of a national state like Japan or China or the broader region as it was once envisioned by "Orientalist" scholars confirms the longstanding practice of keeping their study removed from the wider world of which they are a part and to maintain the quarantine against new theory and methods that would de-ghettoize these "fields." The appeal to native knowledge, even by those who do not qualify as natives, promises to retain the sense of immediacy capable of resisting all mediations. Paul Cohen's earlier call for a sinocentric history of China (an idea whose enunciatory location was the West) reaffirms this desire.[9] If the claims of this unstated hermeneutic rejects theory for the authority of native knowledge and experience, it has also forced its adherents to repeat native pieties and serve willingly as foreign amanuenses interpreting the truths of a native knowledge to their countrymen and women, faithfully conveying the dictations produced on the native ground of cultural authenticity. But this appeal, which still prevails among students of Japan, if not other areas like China and South Asia, contrasts dramatically with the received traditions of studying regions like Europe and Latin America, which are geographically and culturally closer to our own national experience. Unfortunately, Jonathan Culler has recently called for a reorganization of European studies along the lines of this area studies model and its theory of knowledge and thus the repackaging of pedagogy and research as discrete national studies. This is what Adorno once described as a reification of reification, since both the national unit and the multidisciplinary approach to its study succeeded only to reify further a set of practices that long ago lost its enabling purpose.

As a model, area studies have produced a theory of knowledge and its practice based on the authority and authenticity of native experience in a world where the native is no longer on the outside, as once imagined, but, rather, is subjected to the same political-economic processes and structures that all of us encounter in our everyday lives, everywhere and anywhere. The distinction between West and non-West and the privileged geopolitical identification between modernity and a specific place is a Western concept that has been used to establish and maintain Western unity and superiority and can no longer be taken for granted. Any critique must now be positioned not inside or outside the "West," since the West can no longer be thought of as a dominant geographical concept structuring the non-West. Rather, it must be located immanently within the temporality of a modernity embracing new cultural forms that have been and are still developing in what used to be the non-West and that now offer an occasion for dialectical encounter.[10] Owing to its obsessive desire to identify with native knowledge, the practice of area studies risks strangely being linked to more recent efforts to elevate identity and cultural difference as the true vocation of cultural studies seeking to succeed the study of the area. The irony of this move comes with the recognition that area studies have historically sought to separate the study of the home country from its immigrant and diasporic inflections.

The most important consequence of these patterns of identification with the "field" has been to prevent its practitioners from reflecting on themselves as specialists in the field, from seeing the field of practice itself as an object of knowledge production. Instead, it has relied on the natural identification with the native's knowledge and fluency in the cultural idiom as a more than adequate substitute for theoretical self-reflection. But this is simply desire, not a method, which aims to conceal the absence of theory and method that postcolonial studies, the true successor of area studies, have more than satisfied. Such considerations would help explain the intense hostility Japan specialists have shown toward theory and criticism and why they have consistently resisted it.

So far, I've been concerned with the question of why area studies, with its reliance on the unit of the national society, have been notably isolated from other fields of inquiry and categories of research and teaching that validate a self-fulfilling representation. Moreover, in this desire to isolate their knowledge and representations, area studies have overlooked their complicity with a deeply rooted ethnocentrism in the social sciences and humanities.[11] Periodic surveys of the "field" have worked to sustain the identity of the field as such and to give it definition where there has been none, by inventorying personnel, curricula, and institutions. Begun by the SSRC, these surveys have often been indistinguishable from maintaining a system of simple surveillance. In recent years, the Japan Foundation and other Japanese governmental agencies have taken over their funding.

In the most recent survey, supported by the Japan Foundation, one of its organizers reported, without a shred of irony, that Japanese studies, unlike China studies, possess a "remarkable" degree of self-reflection that derives only partially from the "availability of outside financial support" and just as much from the apparent recognition that, quoting the sociologist of Japan R. P. Dore, "area specialists acquire the characteristics of the area they study." "Like our Japanese counterparts," the report continued, "American Japan specialists have acquired the habits of systematic information-gathering and long-range planning."[12] I hope this Japanese genius for planning doesn't include earthquakes, poison gas attacks in subways, and political and financial corruption bordering on incompetence and criminality. This expression of identity belongs to an older model of gathering information in the field that, we're reminded, comes from a time when Japan was "irrelevant" to the United States. If Japan studies were irrelevant in the decades after the war—and I do not believe they were, as I've already explained—it is because they resisted any effort to look beyond the mission attending their inauguration and the representations that best served them. The unintended irony is the belief that Japan studies are now relevant, according to the report, precisely when area studies are being abandoned because they no longer speak to or on, if they ever did, the world we occupy and must try to understand.

While the periodic survey constitutes the sign of surveillance, punctually cementing the identity of the "field," it also calls attention to the larger apparatus of reproduction and the primary role played by funding. In the first reports issued by the SSRC, under the direction of the Joint Committee of Japanese Studies, the funding of and for the "field" became an urgent and early priority. Hall's report, as it was subsequently labeled, pointed to the great strides achieved in the development of Japanese studies in the United States from the end of the war until the 1970s as evidence of momentum that could be sustained only if reliable and stable sources of funding could be identified and tapped.[13] What is striking about Hall's 1970s report, and its successors, is the absence of any attempt to articulate a new or even different intellectual and pedagogical vision that might justify the prioritization of funding.

Following this recommendation, the ensuing search for cash looked to Japan for both public and private sources. A generation of "occupationaires," old Japan hands, and sons of missionaries cashed in their chips, and probably more, to recruit money from both private and public donors in Japan to finance Japanese studies in the United States. This strategy has often gone outside the small world of area studies to encourage business schools, scientific institutions like MIT, and law schools to seek donations for chairs that have nothing to do with Japanese studies as such, but everything to do with Japan. Hence, the resistance to theoretical self-reflection has been compensated by the scramble among proponents of area studies to take money from any willing donor, domestic or foreign, without asking too many questions or worrying too much about finding new ways to think through the more difficult task of constructing a knowledge of Asia and teaching it. The seemingly mad pursuit for endless sources of funding often resembles the campaigns of those earlier adventurers/archaeologists who were always trying to find enough capital to put together one more dig that would complete the picture in some simpleminded positivist fashion, knowing of course, that they were concerned only with getting back to the site and staying there indefinitely. Far from serving any pedagogical or epistemological purpose, the real intention behind this craze to find funding seems to have no other reason than sustaining the structure of area studies and maintaining what can be described only as a dinosaur whose head can longer support its body.

We are reminded by administrators and cooperative academics that universities often claim they are taking money from a foreign government in order to do research, which is always presented as neutral and unaffected by the politics associated with the donor. But this explanation is about as convincing as recent declarations of the president and the Democratic National Committee that financial gifts do not influence policy. Area studies rarely engage in collaborative research projects necessitating large outlays of capital (the last and only significant exception was the University of Michigan's village Japan project), and the kind of individual research being done will still be done without large capital contributions from foreign governments. Princeton University's recent acceptance of money from the Turkish government shows the risks entailed in taking money from a foreign government with a stake in effacing a history of Armenian genocide (fashionably called today "ethnic purification") and the kind of predictable relationship between the expectation of the foreign donor and the willing complicity of American college administrators. The University of California at Berkeley's momentary declaration of intent to name a library after Chiang Ching-kuo—former head of the secret police

in Taiwan, among his many vocations—was simply a repeat performance of the University of Chicago's earlier madness to name
an institute after the Pahlevi family after receiving $2 million in the
early 1960s, which it speedily returned.

Although the search for funding, ostensibly to sustain the structure of area studies and their knowledge and curricula, still characterizes its principal calling, it has also strengthened the resistance to
incorporating new cultural strategies that can resolve the deficien-
cies of an approach driven obsessively by the search for money. This
approach manages only to recuperate the lost historical world of its
own origins as a program of study and research. While the newer cultural studies promise to find new ways to a more productive understanding of how to integrate local experiences into the larger world,
they might also help restore the relevance of national societies by
alerting us to models that will permit researchers to resituate the role
of critique and local experiences as instantiated inflections of larger
processes sharing the same temporality. The importance of cultural
studies is the recognition—completely overlooked by area studies—
of knowledge as production that demands an abandoning of what
Louis Althusser once referred to as the "mirror myths of immediate
vision." If area studies employed a strategy driven by a holistic conception of knowledge—Japan as signified so dear to Japanologists—
and emphasizing enduring cultural values ("core values") and political and social normativity, the method it used was based on a
multidisciplinarism that too often was misrecognized as interdisci-
plinarism. Most area studies programs still presume to cover the
waterfront, which means making sure only that the region in question is approached comprehensively, with all disciplines represented. This means that understanding the area as a totality is possible only when and if all the disciplines are accounted for. Yet this
assumption of this approach to understanding the whole has never
been questioned as long as the disciplinary parts have been lined up
like ducks ready to speak their partial truths. Instead, this strategy
promoted the systematic gathering of information that ultimately
would reflect an invariant reality rather than encourage a critical
practice made possible by producing knowledge from the act of
reading and writing. The one truth that area studies never spoke was

the condition of empowerment that produced a particular knowledge of an area or region to serve the national interest, whether it was the national security state or multinational corporations.

By contrast, the newer cultural studies have tried to break with both holism and a concern for core values in favor of an approach that has consistently turned from knowledge to power and domination. While it has aimed at breaking down disciplinary boundaries to better examine the locus of power and its migrating habits, it has not always managed to replace an earlier and discredited multidisciplinarism. Rather, this obsessive Foucauldianism has often found power everywhere, as well as an opportunity for resistance everywhere. Too often this has resulted in lavish declarations of resistance by the powerless and weak and those consumers who are made to appear as if they are exercising agency when buying a commodity or changing a TV channel. Sometimes the mere enunciation of cultural difference and thus the claim of identity is made to appear as an important political act when it usually signals the disappearance of politics. The politics of identity based on the enunciation of cultural difference is not the same as political identity whose formation depends less on declarations of differences than on some recognition of equivalencies.

All this, however, is an immense improvement over an approach that led its practitioners to acquire the characteristics of the field they study, without thinking about what it meant to invade, inhabit, and "snatch" the body of the other. Because of the implementation of either a Foucauldian desire to locate power everywhere but nowhere specific or a Habermasian dependence on the installation of a public sphere that nobody seems to inhabit yet, the newer cultural studies risk the same reluctance noted in the earlier area studies approach to link power and domination in specific configurations to the role played by capitalism and the state. If the older area studies promoted descriptions masking prescriptives for development in order to export capitalism and its value system to the Third World and to defeat the Second (to open up markets, and so on), the new cultural studies often risk the same by concentrating on microtechnologies and displacing state and capital with indeterminate loci of power and their local variations.

Moreover, they sometimes slip into the role of becoming a cheer-leader for runaway "globalization" and its propensity for border-crossings. The new cultural studies do this by emphasizing dis-courses of power and their slippage, splitting subjectivities, and charting their subsequent dissemination as if the movement were a natural function of an already existing, unnamed conception of social order, even though its practitioners disavow totalities. In more recent efforts to imagine a "globalization" process to account for the local, we see what often appears as a rearticulation of mod-ernization theory in a different register. This neomodernization theory celebrates cultural difference enthusiastically, very much in the manner of the united colors of Benetton yet fails to recog-nize that the production of plural identities is consistent with the propensity of global capitalism to undermine all fixed positions for a fetishized "narcissism of small differences."

Finally, we have the promises offered by postcolonial theory and its desire to account for the complex relationship between col-onizer and colonized, metropole and colony, and chronology and epistemology. It has, first and foremost, given English literary stud-ies a new lease on life once it was recognized that the received canon was too narrow and there were far too few unedited texts to accommodate the swollen army of graduate students recruited in the 1970s and after. In a certain sense, area studies missed the opportunity first made available to them when Edward Said argued in his *Orientalism* that their knowledge of region was already medi-ated by the power/knowledge considerations of colonialism and colonial discourse. Said—correctly, I believe—wanted to assimi-late the practice of area studies to colonial discourse, which would have endowed area studies with a desire to explain the relation-ship between colonizer and colonized, metropole and colony, inside and outside, a world shaped by the forces of Western impe-rialism, as well as the often forgotten observation of Frantz Fanon that hegemonic cultures also colonize the mind.

As for the significant but missed opportunity, it is important to say here that the indifference of area studies to Said's strategic observation meant that they remained locked in their own enclaves of knowledge. The mission of rethinking regions outside Europe, that is, what had become known as the Third World, passed to English studies and the humanities, privileging the textual over the social scientific and the role played by the political economic, even though they shared the older discipline's preoccupation with culture. We should applaud this sensitivity to both the dominated and the margin (nowhere to be found in the older, scientifically "neutral" area studies) and to what Fanon sadly recognized as the "sacking of cultural patterns," or at least its conditions of sacking, in which "the social panorama is destructured; values are flaunted, crushed, emptied."[14] In this regard, postcolonial theory's promise to supply a critique of Eurocentric conceptions of knowledge and provide a forum for the hitherto excluded to speak in their own voice from the margins where domination and power had held them silent since the beginning of modernity—now reread as colonialism—stands as the true successor of area studies, which can be seen as their prehistory. Yet the search for the excluded voice often leads to the futile pursuit for authenticity and restores the Eurocentric claims of the sovereign subject it wishes to eliminate. In this sense, it reveals its own historical myopia and consequent incapacity to see beyond the horizon of a specific colonial encounter—namely, British India—and the retrospective illusion that comes with occupying a position after the colonial moment.

A consideration of the longer duration of history elsewhere would supply examples of different kinds of colonizing and deterritorializing experiences and how the loss of cultural reference, as experienced, say, by the Japanese—even though they did not lose any territory—signified a relationship between colonization and capitalist modernization. Capitalism was seen by the Japanese between the wars as a totalizing process that affected every part of society. This historical experience is crucial to understanding the colonial episode that postcolonial theory currently wishes to theorize. If, for example, this history had been consulted, which actually was contemporary with British colonial rule in India, not to mention Africa and Southeast Asia, it would have shown the impossibility of imagining what Partha Chaterjee has identified as an "anticolonial nationalism" capable of demonstrating that the colonized were not merely, in his memorable words, "consumers of modernity."[15] Chaterjee was suggesting—shared by others who insisted on seeing the availability of uncontaminated autonomous cultures as a reservoir of anti- colonialism—the conviction that the disempowered in India seemed to have involuntarily recuperated the space of nonreification that Lukacs once invested in the proletariat because they were involved in manual, not mental, labor. In making this move, adherents of postcolonial theory misrecognize the identity between capitalism and its claim of universalism; rather, they elide homogeneity with universalism. The point is, as Pierre Vilar reminded us, that capitalism was "born of colonization and the world market" and has subsequently "universalized" history, inasmuch as it has established systematic relations of social interdependence on a global scale that have eventually encompassed noncapitalist societies. In this regard, capitalism has managed to fix a standard of measurement—world time—produced by a "single global space of coexistence," within which action and events are subject to a single, quantifiable chronology. But because different social practices remain outside this abstract measure, capitalism has not "unified" history.[16]

The difference between the Japanese, who were not physically colonized, and the Chinese and Indians, who were, is instructive because they responded to their situation in a way comparable to Chaterjee's description of an uncontaminated anticolonial nationalism, constructing cultural imaginaries rooted in the primacy and authenticity of native cultural patterns and reinventing the culture of reference that Fanon observed had been sacked and emptied. For postcolonial theory, what became the sign of an authentic anticolonial cultural nationalism, uncorrupted by the West, was for the Japanese, Chinese, Indians, French, Germans, and Italians the irreducible mode of a modernist critique of the devastation caused by capitalist modernization and the need to find a location for historical difference. The appeal to native culture was, in fact, the very sign of capitalist modernity and its modernist ideological program rather than resistance to it. The appearance of the uncanny, out-of-time, a ghostly repetition that erupts from the surplus of what had been suppressed to trouble the stable boundaries between past and present, the past in the present, demonstrated that these societies were, in fact, "consumers of modernity" because there appeared to be no other alternative to the de-territorializing wealth of capital and the labor power of the de-territorialized worker. The appeal to such autonomous resources, immune to capitalism even in the colony, is a fiction not worth "delving into," as Fanon recognized long ago.: "A national culture is not a folklore, nor an abstract populism that believes it can discover the people's true nature. It is made up of the inert dregs of gratuitous actions, that is to say actions which are less and less attached to the ever-present reality of the people."[17]

When contemporary postcolonial theory celebrates an anti-colonial nationalism based on an undefiled spirit made to stand as a sign of genuine nativism—uncontaminated interiority—as a form of resistance unmarked by the "consumption of modernity," it is, I believe, unintentionally reviving the response of Japanese modernists to the culture of capitalism in the interwar period. But this repetition, what Raymond Williams named "modernists against modernity," comes now with a difference and a disavowal. In mapping this projection of authenticity onto an earlier moment—the colonial era—they themselves become seekers of the authentic, the inward, the unspoiled, and inadvertently the yearners of a "capitalism without capitalism" and everything that such a gesture implies politically. Moreover, this return to the pursuit of cultural authenticity loops back to form a symmetry with the desire of an earlier area studies program to stand in the place of the native.

Worse, postcolonial theorizing often slips into a kind of necessary ambivalence and indeterminacy that, in the case of Homi Bhabha and Gayatri Spivak, grows out of a methodological desire to exploit the splits and contradictions embedded in the Enlightenment discourse on rationality.[18] Although such a strategy is aimed at unsettling readers and turning them away from the promise of epistemological certainty—because it is a critique that has eschewed consciousness and experience—it is hard to know, unlike the examples of Fanon and Said that show, for whom it is intended and the location of its enunciation. By resorting to the division marked by the colonial experience and its aftermath, it has created a binary no more productive and exempt from charges of essentialism than the older polarities it has held up for derision.

We can recognize the working of this binary in those categories constructed by Homi Bhabha to explain the encounter between the colonizer and the colonized and to signify its complexity. While he was correct to show that the relationship between colonizer and colonized was not simply an instance of a hegemonic discourse representing the other and that this relationship was filled with anxiety and possibilities for slippage, the terms of the encounter still expressed the self and the other recast as pedagogy and performance. Although postcolonial theory has offered through the strategy of compelling dominant structures to restore history as a mediation capable of accounting for differences that older strategies had overlooked, it is, because of the circulation of its own binary terms, often as ahistorical (anahistorical?) and blind to the temporal and spatial differences lived and experienced by those voiceless, excluded, marginalized peoples it seeks to redeem.

The chronology of the colonizer is not always the same for the colonized; Bengal under British rule was different temporally and spatially from Korea under the Japanese, even though they were contemporary, and the forms of colonial domination differ widely from Africa and Asia, demanding sensitivity to the specific political and economic histories that postcolonial theory rarely, if ever, manages to mention. Only history shows the range of such differences and helps us avoid the essentialisms and exceptionalisms that postcolonial theory produces in lifeless stereotypes. In its desire to turn away from the global forces of capitalism—another Western narrative—postcolonial theory trades in stereotypes and holism and the fantasy of genuine, anticolonial nationalism uncontaminated by either the contagion of the colonial epoch or capitalist penetration. It moves ceaselessly from cultural essentialism to an indeterminate social system that need not necessarily be colonial, even though it is named as such, and whose subjects are grasped through a psychoanalytic framework that is culturally specific to the hegemonic culture that the colonized are supposedly trying to resist despite recent efforts to authenticate this psychologizing of other by appealing to the authority of Frantz Fanon as endorsement. With this vacillation, according to Aijaz Ahmad, postcolonial theory has "become transhistorical, always present and always in process of dissolution in one part of the world or another, so that everyone gets the privilege, sooner or later . . . of being colonizer, colonized and postcolonial all at once." Postcolonial theory "levels out all histories, so that we are free to take up any of a thousand of available micro-histories, more or less arbitrarily, since they all amount to the same thing, more or less."[19] We can also employ the power of metonymical example (one of Bhabha's two tropes of fetishism) so that Bengal can stand in for all of Asia or, indeed, the entire colonial world. But if it comes down to this, then postcolonial theory has merely smuggled back the narrative of capitalism under a different name, what Žižek termed a "capitalism without capitalism," that is, capitalism without social divisions, a utopian model of an hybridized globe.

It seems to me that what's left in this endless deconstructive subtraction carried out by postcolonial theory is an innocuous "cultural respect" as its current response to the question of human rights. Now that its initial theoretical splash has turned into a puddle, when researchers have found theory and criticism outside their endless self-referrals, postcoloniality might return to its prehistory in area studies as a step toward enriching both. This would mean coming to grips with postcoloniality's epistemological claims and rewinding them through its original chronological identity as the post to colonialism. By returning to its incipient origins in area studies, postcoloniality might recover the moment when the Third World was viewed from its colonial past but not necessarily from the perspective of its later unwanted heritage—the apparent price it has had to pay for decolonization. This reunion might impose on postcoloniality memories of uneven political-economic and cultural development and a reminder of the powerful presence of capitalism and its secular, historical totalization we call modernity as the principal de-territorializing agent and the determinant of a bounded narrative. By the same measure, postcoloniality might infuse into a moribund area studies the memory of a desire for theory that was early repressed in the scramble to recruit funds rather than ideas. What this points to is how postcoloniality might be refigured into an act of memory rather than merely a chronology or critique masquerading exceptionalisms and unnamed social theories that might help us discriminate among current claims identifying history with memory and restoring to each their own order of knowledge and experience.

Beyond this move to memoration, we might look to a new candidate for cultural studies that would cloak history in the form of everydayness in the larger and immanent framework of capitalist modernity and its transformations. Such a study might redirect our attention to the role of capitalism throughout the world, rather than merely cheering it on or repressing it, and alert us to the relationship between the experience of everydayness and the regime of the commodity form, surely one of the principal agencies of the production of contemporary historical formations. Such a consideration might also allow the current practice of cultural studies in the United States and the United Kingdom to venture beyond its profession of reproducing the kind of Euro-American centrism it was supposed to overcome.[20] Perhaps the time has come, as Žižek proposed, to "resuscitate the Marxian insight that Capital is the ultimate power of 'de-territorialization' which undermines every fixed social identity, and to conceive of 'late capitalism' as the epoch in which the traditional fixity of ideological positions . . . becomes an obstacle to the unbridled commodification of everyday life."[21] Žižek's observation corresponds to DeLeuze and Guattari's earlier reminder (in *Anti-Oedipus*) that capitalism constituted the determining motor of colonialism.

What is important in these cases is that our attention is redirected to capitalism's role in colonialism and, in the case of Žižek, to the relationship between the experience of everydayness and the process of commodification. In this connection, even Homi Bhabha has distinguished between what he labeled the "epochal" and the "everyday" (echoing Henri Lefebvre's earlier pairing of "exceptional" and "everyday"), in which the latter breaks off from the former in order to negotiate the meaning of the modern in "the 'enunciative' present of the discourse." It is in this lag that he proposes "a temporal caesura" that separates the "epochal 'event'" of modernity as the symbol of the continuity of progress, and the contemporaneity of the everyday.[22] Yet the epochal event is merely another way of naming the pedagogical, whereas the everyday becomes the performative, the "time lag," and thus the movable furniture in an endless game of musical chairs attesting to the functions and functioning of an absent social system that is present in its operations. Bhabha also argues that the power of the "performative," its "deformative structure," introduces another "hybrid." But here, as elsewhere, the hybrid merely masks a more corrosive and destructive unevenness that distinguishes the everyday. That is, the realization of hybridity, the "in-betweenness," conceals the mix of elements that are being hybridized and thus works to smooth the experience of unevenness of both the colonized and the non-colonized everyday.

Everyday life refers to the experience of the lived reality that marks the appearance and expansion of industrial capitalism and its propensity to install similar conditions everywhere it is established. Everyday life has the impressive and probably unparalleled credential of standing at the intersection of four intellectual movements that are at the heart of our own, contemporary historical conjuncture: Marxism, surrealism, existentialism (especially its phenomenological perspective), and cultural studies.[23] I am not referring to the conception of the everyday as it was envisioned by Michel DeCerteau in *The Practice of Everyday Life*. Although this conception informs many agendas in cultural studies today, it never has escaped the opening perspective of part 3, which looks down on New York from the heights of the World Trade Tower and makes the topography of the everyday appear as a lifeless, deserted space punctuated by the endless circulation of strategies by the powerful and tactics by the disempowered. This conception also conforms to an unnamed functionalist social conception that permits the expression of forms of resistance that act to defuse the excesses of conflict, like a safety valve, and ensure the maintenance of the social order. Nor am I recalling the everyday that has existed in history since time immemorial which Henri Lefebvre discounted because the prose and poetry of life were still identical.

Because everydayness is different from the daily life lived before capitalism and an epochal modernity, it is, first and foremost, a secular historical concept, a temporality, and not a geopolitical space that until recently—that is, until Japan and then other societies embarked on programs of capitalist modernization—identified modernity with North America and western Europe. In this instance, everydayness constitutes a cultural form that shares with modernity the experience of capitalism and is thus coeval with it. Both are also temporal categories that derive their broader importance from their respective historical forms. Modernity is represented here as the new, and everydayness is seen as the durational present, incomplete but "situated at the intersection of two modes of repetition: the cyclical, which dominates in nature, and the linear, which dominates in processes known as 'rational.'" For Henri Lefebvre, the everyday consists of cycles, nights and days, seasons and harvests, rest and activity, and so forth, and it also requires the repetition of work and consumption. In modernity, work and consumption "masked" and destroyed the cycles. Despite the predictable monotony of repetition, everything changes, especially when control falls into the hands of the "bureaucratic society of controlled consumption" that oversees planned obsolescence. Lefebvre once distinguished between the everyday and the lived—later called modernity and the everyday. The former refers to the global structure or "totality," work, leisure, family life, private life making up the whole yet always marked by its historical, circulating, shifting, and transitory nature. The latter refracts this experience in countless, individual, and contingent ways, attesting to how the everyday is encountered. Everyday life and modernity "crown" and "conceal" the other, "revealing and veiling it." "Everyday life," Lefebvre continued, "a compound of insignificances united in this concept, responds and corresponds to modernity, a compound of signs by which our society expresses and justifies itself and which forms part of its ideology."[24]

Indeed, the "quotidian and the modern mark and mask, legitimate and counterbalance each other." It is the space where the "riddle of recurrence intercepts the theory of becoming."[25] According to Peter Osborne, the incompleteness of the present that Lefebvre believed demanded continuation is, at the same time, an "incomplete de-historicization" that supplies the place of the everyday with the "potential" for rehistoricizing experience."[26] Moreover, this space of everyday life permits us to negotiate relationships between the global and the local, between the rhythms and routines reproduced everywhere that capitalism spreads and the lived or local and contingent experiences mediating them. In this regard, the everyday might function like the Bakhtian chronotope, obliging us to measure the differing relationships between time and space as societies undergo the process of capitalist modernization. "The everyday," according to Lefebvre, "is therefore the most universal and the most unique condition, the most social and the most individuated, the most obvious and the best hidden." It is, as Simmel observed, always immediate, filled with the sedimented layers of countless routines and repetitions that give the present a sense of eternity. But because it always remains incomplete, it is open to the contingent, the unexpected, the eventful, and the possibility for constant refiguration that both time and place necessitate. If the commodification of everyday life leads to de-historicization, we must understand this as a sign of the historical process always found in a specific time and place.

The continuing contradictions among the repetitive cycles that everyday life must constantly negotiate, the ceaseless interactions between modernity and everydayness everywhere, and the refigurations they produce will disclose the operation of that unevenness distinguishing the modern (the regime of the "new") from the cultural forms of everyday life. As different social subjects constantly redefine modernity, these contradictions will also attest to the emergence of new configurations of modernity in what used to be the West and the non-West. In this respect, an examination of everydayness as the site of unevenness will de-privilege the usual cultural emphasis by cultural studies and its text-based orientation for one that at the same time must be sensitive to the materialities of lived political and economic experience. Fredric Jameson alerted us to how cultural studies in the United States is currently a substitute for Marxism and to everything this displacement may imply politically.[27] An appeal to the study of everydayness as the site producing unevenness everywhere will not only remind us of what the practice of cultural studies do not do but also force their practitioners and us to see the relationship of immanently based, different forms of historical temporalization throughout the world. This means that if cultural studies have, as I believe they have, ignored the world outside Euro-America and centered the "articulation" of cultural texts at the expense of political economic considerations, they have done so at the risk of merely recuperating the formalisms they swore to forgo.

At the heart of the everyday life, then, is the figure of uneven development generated by capitalism as it enters societies at different moments and different rates of intensity. Subsequently produced are the differing temporal forms and cultural spaces and the coexistence of differing modes and forces of production. In the 1920s, the Japanese native ethnologist Yanagita Kunio named this combined development "mixed or hybrid civilizations" that could be found throughout East Asia. But he could just as easily have been describing that process everywhere by which modernity and everyday life respond and correspond to each other. What drives this approach is a critical agenda that seeks in the everyday the place where alienations, fetishisms, and reifications produce their effects. While this combined development easily replaces the space occupied by a phantom called Asia—a geographical referent that still fails to conceal its status as the second term—it also shifts our attention away from the singularity of the nation and its counterclaims to uniqueness that, it now seems, are trying to bridge the difference between modernity and everyday life. In a certain sense, it always calls attention to the structure of temporal immanence it shares with other societies even as we concentrate on a local experience. Finally, it will end the long practice of partitioning, which area studies and their principal mode of inquiry—multidisciplinarism—sustained, and their consequent ghettoization in academia to make way for a return to exploring experiences that cross the boundaries of culture areas. For if categories of historical analysis like capital and modernity are to have a particular effect, they will have to be examined in the cultural forms in which history is lived everywhere as a continuing temporalization of existence.[28] But it would have been everydayness, as both Japanese in the inter-war period and Europeans began to realize even before the war, lived as a formation rather than a core value. In this way, it just might be possible to make the transition from area studies to cul-tural studies that DeLillo's hero Gladney made with such dazzling skill from Hitler to Elvis in one easy jump.

2. THE "MYSTERY OF THE EVERYDAY"

Everydayness in History

The everyday: what is most difficult to discover.
— Maurice Blanchot

Among the development of modernities, few examples offer historians a spectacle of greater ambiguity and certainty than Japan's experience in the twentieth century. Sitting at the edge of East Asia, geography saved Japan from the reach of Western colonialism and history and temporarily exempted it from the expansion of the world market. Western traders had gotten as far as Southeast Asia and the South China coast; wars in the Crimea stalled the British, French, and Russian advance; and the United States was preoccupied with its civil war. But if geography and history kept Japan at a distance, they also gave it an opportunity to embark on a transformation that promised to delay indefinitely the imperial and colonial domination experienced by the rest of Asia. Even though Japan was farthest away from the imperial and colonial processes that were incorporating Africa and Asia into the system of industrial capitalism, it was also closest to the figure of modernity exemplified by western Europe and the United States. In the nineteenth century, what was seen to be Asian and backward soon became worldly and modern under the driving force of the Meiji Restoration leading Japan on the path of capitalist modernization and the achievement of parity with the advanced nations of the West. Under the banner of "civilization" and "enlightenment" as the twin goals of state and society, a somnolent Asian feudalism remade itself as modern, which in the nineteenth and early twentieth centuries meant Western.

But if Japanese accomplished the material transformation and secured diplomatic and political recognition earlier and sooner than any country of Europe, it was still seen as a latecomer whose "imitated" achievements remained superficial. This earliest instance of "mimicry" may not have been the ironic resistance imagined by later postcolonial discourse, but it was a doubling that came to desire the status of a subject that is "almost the same but not quite."[1] In the eyes of the West, Japan was still identified with the underdeveloped world; it still lacked the fullness of self that the colonized world was made to affirm by supplying recognition to the West's superiority masquerading as universality. Hence, the ambiguity confronting historians is the problem of accounting for this experience, which either was assimilated into the history of Western modernity as a late but superficial imitation or was seen as a moment in the modernizing process that might permit it to catch up with the West. Maintaining simultaneously its distance and difference, Japan has often been considered an example of both. Both trajectories assumed unlimited progress and the accomplishment of a perfected stage, which meant that countries like Japan and other "latecomers" would defer parity until the last instance, which would never come. We can see traces of this ambiguity in both Japanese who have studied their modern history and non-Japanese who, more often than not, have unwittingly sustained the imperial but contradictory plot line of development, whether Spencerian or Marxian.

In interwar Japan, a vigorous discourse carried out in the mass media, opinion magazines, and even the movies identified the contemporary lived experience as "modern life" and the everyday of the large cities as the distinctive place where it all was occurring. Most thinkers and writers interested in the phenomenon of "modern life" saw the experience as similar to what was taking place in the metropolitan centers of the industrial West. The Japanese philosopher Tosaka Jun perceptively advised that Japan constituted a link to the larger world of modernity, not an exception, and writers returning from extended stays in Europe invariably compared the everyday in Japan with what they had just observed in Paris, London, and Berlin. What for Japanese seemed to be a lived experience in the present that had appeared as a moment in the "opening of the historical process" was later refigured by historical sociology into an empirical category narrating a process that marked breaks and ruptures in the development schema of societies, which in the late 1950s was called *modernization theory*.[2]

This view of the world presupposed an underlying unity of a period that would sort out and differentiate at a number of levels political and legal forms, religion and cultural organization, social structures, and individual psychology. In the intellectual and scholarly world of area studies, modernization theory was used to identify as late developers all those regions that industrialized after western Europe and the United States did or those colonial realms whose development remained subordinated to that of their home countries and recast these societies in an airless framework of development and homogeneity across historical time. Accordingly, American social science occupied a position from which to make comparative judgments about the location and social development of the "non-West" without considering any qualitative temporal differences. But unlike the minimal unity afforded by the category of everydayness, modernization neglected experience for structure and development.

The modern life of the present lived earlier by Japanese was resituated on this developmental trajectory. An earlier binary that classified the West as whole and developed and the rest as fragmented and incomplete was refigured into a conception of evolutionary adaptation and development and an export model of growth. In the scholarly world of the 1960s and 1970s, this strategy dominated area studies' research agendas, as I've already noted, and its most spectacular example was Japan. Its most disappointing failure was a decolonized India and the social residues of a precolonial tradition that blocked the path of successful economic and political modernization. With India, modernization enthusiasts momentarily saw an opportunity for an Asian success story—nonrevolutionary political and economic development—capable of supplying a political alternative to the revolutionary model exemplified by the People's Republic of China. Behind this conviction was the misrecognition of modernization theory that linked decolonization to Great Britain's tutelage as the necessary condition for what was called a successful take-off. Instead, the example of India was transmuted into an instance of postcolonial misery that was eventually extended beyond its original referent to include all formerly colonized societies in order to constitute a new narrative. This was driven by a binary logic that questioned the relationship between colonizer and colonized to explain why the formation of the former was incomplete without considering the latter.

Despite the differences, modernization theory and its postcolonial successor share the presumption of a homogeneous continuum of historical time that enables abstracted comparative judgments free from qualitative temporal differences. Both, but especially modernization theory, fail to acknowledge that modernity, tradition, past and present, are categories of "historical totalization in the medium of cultural experience," demanding, therefore, distinct forms or ways of temporalizing history through which the developmental stages—lived time—are bonded together in the unity of a single, historical view. Peter Osborne has noted that such temporalizations are usually associated with particular epistemologies (which disclose temporal forms and the limits of knowledge) and thereby reveal particular orientations toward practice, what he has called the "politics of time."[3]

Since modernity, tradition, and postcoloniality are seen as interventions in the field of political time, it is important to distinguish among historical studies of "cultural forms" that both modernization theory and postcolonial discourse usually group under a single or homogeneous historical continuum. What modernization has obscured—and this was partly shared by Marxists of an earlier economistic persuasion—is the idea of modernity as a specific cultural form and a consciousness of lived historical time that differs according to social forms and practices. They themselves depend as much on the experiences of place as they do on time. In part, these differences were marked by the way modernity was eventually differentiated from the space of everydayness. Because modernity marked the present as a minimal unity and thus as the intersection between the new and the residual stemming from a different time, histories, and cultural conventions, it made possible the production of differing inflections of the modern. It also promised not alternative modernities but coeval or, better yet, peripheral modernities (as long as peripheral is understood only as a relationship to the centers of capitalism before World War II), in which all societies shared a common reference provided by global capital and its requirements. Each society, however, differed according to specific times and places, the "not quite the same."[4] (Capitalism always differed wherever it established its regime, despite the putative similarity of its procedures and processes.)

In this regard, modernity provided a framework of temporal imminence in which to locate all societies. This was a conception of modernity rarely, if ever, imagined by classic theorists like Durkheim, Weber, and Simmel. If modernity was driven by the desiring machine of capitalism, promising to install its regime of production and consumption everywhere, the everyday, serving as a minimal unification of the present and signaling the level of lived experience and reproduction would, in fact, negotiate the compelling demands of homogeneity through the mediations of a past that constantly stood in a tense, often antagonistic, relationship to the present of the new.

Japan's transformation into a modern order, along with other societies moving at different paces elsewhere in places peripheral to the world of Western capital, revealed early the fiction that modernity was solely a Western idea, that the imposed dyad of West and non-West (note the negativity of this name) and everything else it implied should determine the geographic location and perspective of modernity. Owing to its earlier and rapid modernization, Japan, when compared with China and societies in Southeast Asia and the Middle East, showed that this identification of the geopolitical West as the place of modernity merely established and maintained its unity and superiority. Once Japan seized on modernization and fought a successful war against a Western nation, the geopolitical monopoly of modernity was shattered, even though opinion continued to assume that Japan was simply a copy.

The spell of a spatial configuration of modernity between a civilized West and an ethnographic non-West was finally broken, and new configurations of modernity began to emerge throughout the world whose experiences did not always or necessarily conform to a model demanding homogenization. This modernity, as Japan showed, was marked by the formation of a space of everyday life rooted in a specific location yet connected to a broader context of space/time. The place of everyday life signified only one among many manifest possibilities and thus a moment in the network of social relationships and understanding. This meant that everydayness, as it was formed in the great metropolitan centers like Tokyo/ Yokohama, Shanghai, Calcutta, and Rio De Janeiro, included relations that stretched far beyond the borders and experience of a singular locale, reaching a new kind of unboundedness, in which space was increasingly torn away from place by "fostering relations between 'absent' others." In Japan, the experience of everydayness was revealed as "phantasmagoric," inasmuch as the locale—place—was penetrated and shaped by practices and knowledges distant and distinct from those received from an immediate history and culture.[5] The coexistence of different forms of economic life came to signal an experience that was both modern and distinct, sanctioning an unevenness that capitalist political economy had made as a principal condition of its expansion, even though it would seek to repress it in claims of even development everywhere.

This conception of everydayness was formulated and lived within a discourse on modernity that developed as a commentary on the formation of a modern, capitalist society in Europe in the nineteenth century. While it was not always or consistently found as an object of explicit theorization, eluding direct analysis because of its multiple, diffuse, and ubiquitous appearances, it was, nevertheless, clearly identified by the major theorists of modernity. Even so, a direct and explicit theorization of everyday life came after World War II with Henri Lefebvre's formulation of critique, Gaston Bachelard's identification of the centrality and unity of the "house" as an example of the poetics of space, Edgar Morin's site of contested modernization, Michel DeCerteau's reworking of it as a space, and German labor historians like Alf Luedtke who, dissatisfied by the macrocosmic claims of social history (not to mention the negative associations produced by Heidegger and the lived existence identified with the Nazi period) turned to the experience of the worker and the workplace. What the German inflection represented was the effort to dissolve the separation between bourgeois everydayness and the domain of the laborer in order to show that workplace and worker were at the heart of any definition of the everyday.[6]

In the United States, there was the early work of Irving Goffman, who saw everyday life as an endless stage in which people perform representations of roles necessary for the functioning of the social system, and Dorothy Smith, who refigured everyday life as a problematic, as she put it, to account for women's experience which was often neglected; yet she questioned the claim that this sphere represented the private and the realm of reproduction.[7] To be sure, thinkers since Marx have treated everyday life as an object of reflection and seriousness. For Europeans, the status of everydayness, and its temporality, was juxtaposed to the structure of modernity and public time and was thematized by writers like Joyce, Kafka, and Proust and philosophers like Bergson. "Hold to the now," Stephen Daedalus demands, "the here, through which all future plunges to the past."

In Japan, as I will try to show, the idea of everydayness was seen as part of this experience of accelerated modernization in the interwar period and became a principle driving theorization and discourse at a pace of intensity quite unlike that of the European response. The reason for this difference stems in part from the specular contrast between imported customs and practices identified with foreign cultures, and received and homegrown conventions put into question by the introduction of the new. This process was less sharply differentiated among European societies, which were more closely bound together and shared long histories of cultural contact and interchange, except for the new Soviet Union, which stood in dramatic contrast to the capitalist cities of the West and to its own rural past that coexisted with the new. Instead, the European experience was noted for the acceleration of the modernization process as it spread to cities like Berlin, where the swelling of the population and its attendant changes occurred in a very short period of time. This process gained strength in the decade immediately before World War I and sped ahead in the following decades. This was especially true of regions and countries on the periphery of the industrial center, like Japan and the

Soviet Union and the colonized and semicolonized societies in Asia and Latin America. For the Japanese, and presumably other societies outside Europe and North America, the rapidity of this development was underscored by the jarring encounter with the new that came from elsewhere.

The appearance of new industrial and financial cities in Tokyo and Osaka and throughout the industrializing world of the 1920s occurred in a "historical conjuncture" characterized by the establishment of new industries producing peacetime consumer commodities, the development of new public and private financial institutions, the emergence of new constituencies, the formation of new subject positions, and gender and sexual identities that actualized the conditions for configuring a distinctive ideology and its numerous variations called modernism. A genuine transnational concept that unified multiple cultural forms throughout the industrializing world, modernism constituted a temporal logic based on the "new." This modernism (or modernisms) was increasingly expressed through the cultural optic of what, in the 1920s, was known as "Americanism." Everywhere in the industrializing world, from Paris to Tokyo, the appeal to "Americanism" signified the new, speed, technology, and new modes of producing commodities. Just as an Italian playwright like Pirandello could announce in 1929 that "Americanism is swamping us. I think a new beacon of civilization has been lit over here,"[8] the Japanese writer and playwright Kikuchi Kan could confidently declare two years earlier that Americanism marked the beginning of modernity and a new civilization in Japan. The Soviet constructivist Boris Arbatov looked to America as the source of new production methods that would transform Russia's cities and everyday life. While this effusive celebration of Americanism was usually an expression of desire more than an ubiquitous reality that was being lived, it nevertheless attested to an emerging historical situation dominated by the figure of modernism in the arts and an outlook that was repudiating an antecedent past for an endless present no longer distinguishable from the future. No figure throughout the industrializing world was more empowering than "Americanism," which referred to both hegemony of technological production—what

Gramsci identified as "Fordism," however exaggerated its implementation in only a few consumer industries and limited its geographical range—and greater commodification in everyday life. Although the response to this new cultural force could elicit a diversity of responses, from Arbatov's enthusiastic approval through Walter Benjamin's elaboration of the importance of mechanical reproduction to Ōya Sōichi's[9] denunciation of its superficiality and diluting properties, its presence in everyday life in the industrializing world could not be denied.

As social theorists everywhere were already discovering, Americanism was a present caught between trying to sever its relationship to the past and seeking to envision an indeterminate future that resembled an endless present producing the very-new in the ever-same. The chronology of this moment was bounded by the years immediately before World War I and its aftermath and the beginning of World War II (even though some who have worried about the starting point of a distinctive postmodernity wish, to carry modernism into its decline in the years after World War II), the reign of commodity-producing technologies and mass consumption, and the war's aftermath and the interwar years. Modernization was characterized by the coexistence of different economies—capitalist, precapitalist, and socialist—and the continuous clash of conflict of political and social forces reflecting the claims of the past and the future. Capitalist modernization and the growing centrality of the market had already become an organizing principle for new social relationships everywhere, except in the Soviet Union, and had redefined a daily life vastly different from what had been known and lived in the recent past.

The historian Arno Mayer perceptively named this unstable political context after World War I the "persistence of the old regime," which refers to the continuing empowerment of traditional, agrarian-based leadership in European societies committed to capitalist and industrial transformation.[10] While he could easily have been describing Japan, it is interesting to note that Japan's modernization in the 1920s often resembled what was being envisaged in the Soviet Union, as Japanese thinkers momentarily employed the theoretical apparatus of Russian avant-gardists to express their own social aspirations. The idea of a shared historical conjuncture marking the moment of massive capitalist modernization prompted Siegfried Kracauer to remark, somewhat optimistically in the 1920s, that "the metropolitan centers were becoming more and more alike and their differences are disappearing."[11]

If it is true that capitalist modernization initially swept away everything in its path, giving greater force to the trope of "Americanism," the continued de-territorialization, driven by large-scale migrations from the countryside to the centers of production and consumption, swiftly and often definitively destroyed all received systems of reference. In the early twentieth century, the Japanese critic Yokoi Tokiyoshi was already calling this ceaseless flow from the countryside to the cities "city sickness" (toshibyō), and Georg Simmel was trying to identify the specific effects of metropolitan life on social relations and psychological disposition. Everywhere capitalism established its arrangement of production and its productive authority, it sacked inherited cultural patterns; questioned and sometimes eliminated their enabling conditions; undermined existing social bases; and flaunted, crushed, and emptied familiar values, customs, and practices that had regulated the rhythms of received life. Colonialism, physical and military and mental and cultural, went even further in pursuing this de-territorializing program by employing forms of voluntary and involuntary violence. As a result, the cities developed at a much faster rate than the countryside, which often was made to supply both capital and labor for their growth. In this regard, the countryside and the colony shared the affliction of being "sacrificed," as Yanagita Kunio recognized in the late 1920s, for the "splendors" of the city.[12] By the end of the 1930s in Japan, writers and thinkers were describing their condition as "diseased" and their circumstances of cultural confinement as one that corresponded to a "madhouse."

In the great industrial transformation of the early twentieth century, whether capitalist or socialist, the experience of the present was organized and unified in the conception of the everyday. If in the capitalist countries of the West, we could see through the routine and commonality of everyday life as it was being lived and experienced in the cities to find an as yet unrealized promise for a more humane and just society, the Soviets were looking at the life of the industrial proletariat for the possibility of a new order that could liberate itself from the baggage of bourgeois culture and its fascination with the new and the pleasures once associated with working-class life in the nineteenth century.[13] But, we should add, everydayness was seen, even outside the Soviet Union, as promising to disclose the possibility of a more human form of existence and to identify a different order of things free from the constraints of commodification and social abstraction.

In his *Psychopathology of Everyday Life* (1901),[14] when Freud first identified the everyday as the place where slips in speech symptomized deeper, buried meanings, he paralleled but went further than Marx, who saw in the phenomenality of immediate conditions the significations of deep and undisclosed social structures authorized to direct the movement of the surface. For Freud, nothing was insignificant, and the most mundane speech situation could have unsuspected meanings. In this way, the everyday was made the site of both multivariate and complex expression, despite the seeming routinization of its surface, and the object of scientific research and political intervention. Hence, the everyday acquired the association of a "dynamic social reality" rather than merely the ordinary and prosaic.[15] With this transformation, the everyday in the 1920s — virtually everywhere industrialization had been established — was no longer simply the place of positivistic facticity but the space where common experience concealed deeper conflicts and contradictions whose elucidation was available to a rational consciousness. Rather than being an inert experience of facts, everyday life was increasingly seen as the site that revealed symptoms of societies' deepest conflicts and aspirations. In the years following the war, "modern life" was transmuted everywhere into the everyday, denoting a significant shift away from the merely new and novel to the concreteness of lived experience in the cities where reification was producing its effect and where new, political, and cultural possibilities were being sought.

In Japan, for example, what was first described as *"modan raifu"* (modern life) in the immediate postwar period was used interchangeably with the neutral term *seikatsu* (life, living) but was

refined into "everyday ordinary life" (*nichijō seikatsu*) and ultimately configured into a space where possibility was seen to inhere
in routine, habit, and custom. This naming, in Japan and everywhere else the everyday unified the present, exemplified an effort
to identify an experience that was buffeted by the modern and new
but was still able to remain distinct. Everyday life represented a
concern for the actual, as both Walter Benjamin and Tosaka Jun
observed, which meant actualizing the historical present—the
now—in order to extract from it lost and forgotten promises of the
past and possibilities for the future. A very real part of actualizing
the now required an immense act of mourning and remembering
that was able to recall the past whose promise the present had
repressed. Often this act of remembrance slid into forms of nostalgia for a cultural mastery attributed to an indeterminate past
now cast as an alternative to the dangers posed by a performative
present. What the actual referred to was not simply the facticity of
present existence but, rather, the actualization of concrete experience that would lead to a different present, that would, as Benjamin explained, fill in the vacated now of recognizability. If everydayness was a minimal unity organizing the present, it also opened
up to multiple ways of unifying experience, aligning the everyday
with art or politics, and thus pledging to seal the divisions of contradictions menacing the present.

In this context, we have the examples of John Roberts, who
explained how the contestation of representations of everyday life
in the new Soviet Union disclosed how the everyday could unify
time and space in specific modalities; or Adrian Rifkin,[16] who
showed the unifying power of linking songs and popular pleasures
to the everyday life of the working class in interwar France; or
Kristin Ross,[17] who demonstrated in France in the 1960s how the
division spawned by decolonization and war in Algeria was re-
paired in a new conception of middle-class everydayness centered
in the modernization of social life, cars, clean bodies, and the life
of new professional cadres. In Japan, the work of Gonda Yasunosuke before the war linked popular culture and leisure to work and
called attention to the necessary coexistence of traditional pleasures and performance and the new entertainments among the

working class in the larger cities. More recently, Michael Dutton has demonstrated how "street life" in post-Mao China, while constituting a moving montage, still manages to unify everyday life.[18]

What distinguished the discourse on everydayness was how often it concentrated on the details of multiple practices, starting with unimportant, shallow, and trivial occurrences. "The place which an epoch occupies in the historical process," Siegfried Kracauer wrote in the *Mass Ornament*, "is determined . . . in the analysis of its insignificant, superficial manifestations than from the judgment of the epoch upon itself" (p. 75). In his *Die Angestellten*, he observed during his visits to the labor court how aggregate facts of the economic life of employees determined the conditions of their existence. But he also reminded himself of the necessity of ridding "ourselves of the delusion that is the major events of history that determine men." Rather, it is the small catastrophes in everyday life that lastingly influence employees' lives and the "miniaturized events" that affect their fate.[19] This is what Georg Simmel earlier called "momentary images," "snapshots" constituting the "individual threads" of social reality. Earlier theorists like Marx, Weber, and Durkheim concentrated on analyzing the social totality rather than the modes of experiencing a reality that was fleeting, transitory, and arbitrary. Even Georg Lukacs, who was perhaps the most forceful interpreter of how everydayness becomes reified, wanted to show this phenomenon under the sign of the totality, not in the register of moments of experience.[20] Often this tactic led to seeing a singular experience or manifestation as a metonym of larger and unarticulated wholes, much like Joyce's narrative of a day in the life of Leopold Bloom or what Kracauer called "quotations or observations on the spot . . . [that] are not to be taken as instances of this or that theory but as exemplary cases of reality."[21] More familiar, Walter Benjamin defined these flashing moments as "dialectical images."

By contrast, the great social theorists like Marx, Durkheim, and Weber sought to chart the shape of totalities like the social or primary institutions as fixed and secure objects of examination through which they could analyze the modern. This impulse partly explains why Marxists, especially, were slow to regard the experience of everyday life as a coherently worthy subject of investigation and instead looked to the larger structures of the social totality whose behavior would reveal the impending collapse of the capitalist mode of production and its social formation. Structures offered entry to concrete and material reality while experience was often relegated to ideological reflection. In this sense, the everyday was subsumed under capitalism and modernity, consciousness and experience frozen in a reified state that, according to Lukacs, only the proletariat—despite being transformed into the figure of a "de-humanized" commodity atrophying the "soul"—was still able "to rebel against reification," unlike the bureaucrat whose "thoughts" and "feelings" had been objectified through and through.[22] (I should point out that to Heidegger, this reified state was transformed into an inauthentic everydayness, the world of *das Man.*)

The process of commodification reduced the present successively toward instantaneity, endless simultaneity, the new in the ever-same (Husserl's "retentional" source), and produced a de-historicization of life, "within which events are consumed as images, independently of each other, and without narrative connection."[23] Too often, thinkers like Weber, Simmel, and Kracauer submitted to the temptation to see everyday life as a perennial present, instants successively piled on top of one another, as Tosaka Jun imagined, assuming the de-historicized coloration of the commodity, seeing the products of this experience of capitalism as culturally unspecific, indeterminate, and homogenizing everywhere, strangely akin to capitalism's ideological representation of itself. Heidegger went even further to formulate a different conception of historicization—called historicality—that revealed the negativity of everyday life as spurious and historically false—the site of inauthenticity. But by rethinking everyday life and history and their relationship, he put them in the foreground in any subsequent consideration of modernity and its temporality. Before the war, only Benjamin and possibly the Portuguese poet Fernando Pessoa, owing to their admiration for surrealism, saw in the everyday the mystery of its difference, the watermark of a history concealed under the smooth surface of routine and sameness. Yet it should be pointed out that a number of Japanese writers were proclaiming that they had discovered in the place of everyday life the sign of its history, a crystallization of historical temporality embedded in the space of everyday life, an accumulation of successive todays, as it was put, distinct from the realm of possibility available to it still capable of animating moments of difference and promising that tomorrow would not be the same as today.

If Marx grasped modernity as a historical formation devoted to the new, he also recognized that the new was a transitory phenomenon. But it was Weber, I believe, who fixed firmly the geographic location of this historical phenomenon in the West and constructed a vast historical sociology, more spatial than temporal, that established the modern everyday in a specific place and linked it to the process of rationalization (the other side of reification) which capitalism best exemplified. Weber separated the routinization of everyday life brought on by rationalization from the religious, which increasingly became the domain of non-everyday life, capable of escaping its dominations, and the sources of spirituality, which supposedly could account for motivation, meaning, and behavior in the everyday. What lay behind his scheme, fundamental to Simmel, was the presumed division of an objective, empirical world and the existence of an inner realm independent of or separable from concrete, historical life. (We have seen its postcolonial recuperation in writers like Chaterjee.) The former was seen as inalterable, and the latter as the source of motivation, not to change the order, but to serve it out of transcendental duty. In the formulation of a specific ideology, Lukacs saw the relationship between a "revolutionary religiosity of the sects" and the service to the outside world of capitalism. "For the union," he wrote, "of an inwardness, purified to the point of total abstraction and stripped of all traces of flesh and blood, with a transcendental philosophy of history, does indeed correspond to the basic ideological structure of capitalism."[24] In fact, the separation of the everyday world of rational utility and routine and the space of the non-everyday inwardness reinforced the separation of theory and practice, means and end. But both Weber and Lukacs overlooked how easily the everyday might avoid becoming the site of a complete and thorough rationalization of life by presuming capitalism's success as the promoter of even, rather than uneven, development.

If Weber problematized everydayness as separate spheres that he tried to join by appealing to a theory of vocation—a calling (*Beruf*)—Georg Simmel accepted it as an enabling condition of modernity itself and the permanent character of lived existence. To him, the "temporary," the "fugitive," and the "contingent" posed an immense methodological problem: how to grasp as an object of analysis what, in fact, was transitory and fleeting. More important, Simmel was convinced, unlike Marx, that the transitory and the fleeting did not lead to successive stages of development revealing the experience of modernity as a specific form of historical temporality. In his massive *The Philosophy of Money*, Simmel concentrated on the present as the culmination of all preceding pasts or as the way station to a history not yet lived or experienced. Kracauer, who was devoted to Simmel, believed that Simmel lacked a "grand style of grasping history. The interpretation of historical events is foreign to him, and he takes little account of the historical situation in which people find themselves at any given moment" (*MO*, p. 225). The phenomena that Simmel examined have no apparent historicity, no recognizable temporality, but possess only an existence that reveals their connection with all other things in the world. The world portrayed in *The Philosophy of Money* is that of capitalism, even though it is never named or historicized in the slightest but driven by money, exchange, and the production of value, as if it had left history altogether for an unbounded temporality, an endless present.

At the heart of this present, Simmel perceived a growing conflict between objective and subjective cultures, between an accelerating everydayness and the experience of the individual who was found increasingly incapable of staying abreast of and understanding the empirical domain. Money and exchange drove this process of objectification, reifying the "external activities of the subject,"[25] expressed as abstract value "nothing but the relativity of subjects" (*PM*, p. 121). Because money expresses the value relationship between goods, measures them and facilitates their exchange, "it enters the world . . . as a power of entirely different origins" (p. 122). Simmel saw money as the cause separating the objective and subjective realms. "The metaphysical sublimation of value," he proposed, "does not play any role in the valuations of daily life, which are concerned only with values in the consciousness of the subject." Value develops with the increase in distance between the consumer and "the cause of his enjoyment," which he defined as desire. "The possibility of enjoyment must be separated, as an image of the future, from our present condition in order for us to desire things that now stand at a distance from us." Distance, echoing Nietzsche's "aristocratic pathos," now described the growing gap between desire and attainability (p. 69).

Simmel's attention in this divided world was caught by the mode employed by the individual subject in experiencing everyday life, a world of floating and fleeting fragments, not the extraordinary life "but rather an everyday existence and each of its nameless moments."[26] Even though he saw an objective, empirical realm outpacing the individual subject's capacity to understand it fully, he was convinced that subjective culture "exists only if man draws into his development something that is external to him."[27] For Simmel, it was axiomatic that the external world, however distant, would, at some point, enter the inner life, the "soul," as he put it, and affect its formation. What counted as lived experience was not so much one of raw, unmediated materiality but, rather, one that had been mediated, shaped, and worked over by what he called "inner nervosity," which meant incorporating the fleeting fragments into an inner life. In this way, he could be seen moving away from the actual site of everyday life as a concrete place to engage and directly experience (*Erlebnis*) whose many meanings conveyed a sense of "seeing" and to draw closer to a memory of the experience, a doubly reified encounter with the now so as to buoy the inner subjective domain against the objective and objectifying world running ahead of the individual (*PM*, p. 450). In other words, Simmel was opposed to simple reflection.

Just as everyday life is surrounded more and more by objects of which we cannot conceive how much intellectual effort is expended in their production, so our mental and social communication is filled with symbolic terms, in which a comprehensive intellectuality is accumulated but of which the individual need make only minimal use.

This constituted the domination of the objective world over "subjective culture," a "discrepancy" that "everyday and from all sides the objective culture increases but the individual mind can enrich the forms and content of its development only by distancing itself still further from that culture and developing its own at a much slower pace" (PM, p. 449).

In the "Metropolis and Mental Life," Simmel identified the city, and especially its streets, as the place of "tempo and multiplicity of economic, occupational and social life" (GS, p. 325) and as the temporality when the intensification of creational activity and the discrepancy caused by the division of labor is greatest. The great cities force their inhabitants to resist the "overgrowth of objectification" and their propensity to absorb the individual, so as to "become a single cog . . . in the vast overwhelming organization of things and forces . . . which gradually take out of his hands everything connected with progress, spirituality and value" (p. 337). The last defense against the tidal wave of objective existence—which Simmel explained as homogenization—and the worrisome disappearance of "subjective form" was the recesses of the inner life.

It was thus in the city that Simmel observed the consequences of the expanding money economy and how it engulfed everyday existence. In The Philosophy of Money, according to Lukacs, Simmel believed that the material content of everyday life should become all the more material and impersonal in order to guarantee the personalized character of the "non-reifiable remnant" and the indubitable property of the person. This meant recognizing the absence of mediations that might permit understanding the relationships between the two separate spheres. For Simmel, the "very thing" that should be understood "with the aid of mediation" ends up becoming the accepted principle used to explain all phenomena. Elevated to the status of value, Lukacs continued, the "unexplained" and "inexplicable facticity of bourgeois existence" in the here and now acquires the appearance of an eternal law of nature or acts like a cultural value capable of enduring for all time.[28] Modern man, Simmel conceded, is so surrounded by nothing but impersonal, lifeless objects that he becomes more and more obliged to accept the idea that he is living in an anti-individualistic social order. "Cultural objects increasingly evolve into an interconnected enclosed world that has . . . fewer points at which the subjective soul [*Geist*] can interpose its will and feelings" (*PM*, pp. 459–461). Objects and people have become estranged from one another (p. 460).

Even the fortunate modern who is able to secure an island of subjectivity, "a secret closed off sphere of privacy," does so because money "relieves" us from direct "contact with things" (p. 469). Money was, in fact, Simmel's substitute for mediations that might explain the separation that had eternalized the present (pp. 485, 484). Under the sanction of conditions he called "constancy," history must disappear. Modern life, driven by money and exchange, has destroyed all natural "periodicities," since the "leveling effect of culture" ensures the availability of all the necessities of life throughout the year. It destroys the idea of everything in its own time, since it is possible to "buy anything at any time for money." Hence the emotions and stimulations of the individual need no longer follow a "rhythm that would enforce a periodicity in order to satisfy them" (p. 487). The implications of this destruction of patterned periodicity meant that culture had overcome both time and space and that definite periods of time no longer determined the framework for activities. Rather, "they now depend only upon the relationship between the will and our ability and upon the purely objective conditions for carrying them out" (p. 488). In this world, time was pressed into a present that obeyed no real differentiations, in which temporality itself is freed from the boundedness of past, present, and future. History was reduced to the image of an ever-present everyday life no longer marked by periodicities but only by the repetition of "will," "ability," and the "objective conditions for carrying them out." The past existed only in its traces, as Simmel explained elsewhere, which could be found in the survival of the "ruin," now standing in the landscape of modern life as a reminder of a vanished moment before the separation between objective and subjective realms was permanently frozen to produce a perpetual present and its "strong sense of presentness."[29] Without saying so, Simmel's present was the timeless world of the commodity.

Despite this early recognition in western Europe by thinkers as diverse Simmel and Lukacs of the necessity of piercing through the crust of the commodity form in order to locate meaning and possibility in the new urban everydayness, this problem was for a moment deferred to the new society of the Soviet Union. In the early and "carnivalesque" years of the New Economic Policy and exciting experimentation in the arts throughout the 1920s until the advent of Stalinism, the problem of capitalist commodification and the status of the object was inverted in such a way as to provide the vision of a new technical but human order, rational but unreified. John Roberts has proposed that the Russian Revolution sharpened the conception of the everyday because it was the first society in history in which the worker was put in charge of social reality.[30] For this reason, the everyday in Soviet society was open to greater politicization than in the industrial states of the West, as its very newness appealed to modernizing societies further to the east, such as Japan, where thinkers and activists drew their inspiration from the social experiments to prepare for both reconstruction and possible revolution in their own society. The unprecedented newness of the Japanese experience contributed as well, as it was not long emerged from the feudalism it overthrew in 1868 and equipped with the infrastructure of a modern society Meiji leadership carefully implanted by the time of World War I. In 1924, Leon Trotsky hurriedly wrote a book on the new Soviet everyday which presented an inventory of the problems encountered in building a new society during a time of civil war.[31]

More systematic theorizing came with the writings of a radical productivist and former member of the Proletkult, Boris Arbatov, and later in the meditations of Bakhtin and Voloshinov. Responding to the Proletkult's left-wing requirements to unify art and everyday life under the sanction of the production process, Arbatov looked beyond the seductions of "good design," which he identified with the residues of bourgeois artisanal art and the lingering conceits of art for art's sake. According to his principal work, *Art and Production* (1927), it was necessary for the proletariat to eliminate the "historically determined barrier between artistic technique and general social technique."[32] It is interesting that this program was nearly identical with the proposals of the Japanese artist/thinker Murayama Tomoyoshi and his group of devoted constructivists (MAVO).[33] Arbatov proposed replacing the expressivist and individualistic aesthetic mentality that had directed artisanal production since the last century with one that promised to reunite individual production and everyday life. In his conception of everyday life, there would be no distinction between artist and worker, no gulf separating the use value of things from their exchange value. This program was at the heart of an earlier essay entitled "Everyday Life and the Culture of the Thing" written in 1925, which offered an original account of nonreified consumption in a socialist society, even as it adhered to the received identification of production, technology, and art.[34] Envisioning the object capable of becoming "something functional and active," in contrast to the experience of Western capitalism in which the object had already suborned social relations and was establishing a regime of social abstraction, Arbatov was convinced that the thing behaved much like a "co-worker with human practice" (Arbatov, p. 126). Like his Japanese contemporary the urban researcher Kon Wajirō, Arbatov believed that rather than acting as the agent of objectification, the thing could reinforce productive subjectivity. Because modern society was powered by the production of objects in its daily transactions, which fed back into the productive sphere, people acquired their subject positions through the countless use of things. This was the same tactic adopted by Kon in his conceptualization of new subject positions, which were formed as a result of buying and using diverse things.[35]

Seeking a way to think of production in a new socialist society outside those constraints that in the West oppressed work and the worker, Arbatov was convinced that because "material culture is the production and consumption of material values," culture is thus created by all the "material forces, just as society's cultural style is created by all of its construction" (Arbatov, p. 120). Mediating this relationship of individual and collectivity is the "thing," which occupies a singularly important position in any materialist conception of life, even though it has been imperfectly understood by most Marxists who have not been liberated from the bourgeois world of things. Here, Arbatov's conception of new understanding of the thing appeared as a replay of his critique of bourgeois artisanal art and its separation from life. Blinded by a view that insisted on dividing the technical from everyday things into distinct realms, the everyday failed to attract serious "scientific consideration" and was dismissed as a "static and secondary form." The consequences of this bourgeois blindness overlooked this world of things as both material process and forms that separate social consciousness and practice from the materiality of objects. Confident that the construction of a truly socialist culture organized by the working class would repair the "rupture" between things and people that persisted as a residue of an older bourgeois order, proletarian life would try to destroy this destructive dualism for a "single methodological" perspective that saw the world of things as an all-encompassing material entity that produced forms. Society had not yet reached this level of development. But recognizing the importance of relating things to people would, Arbatov believed, reveal the essentials of the emerging proletarian culture.

His argument was based on the conviction that "material forms of culture" were actually figures "detached" as "skeletal formations," representing a "conservative force" known as the everyday-*byt*.[36] The task was to move this conservative everyday life into the site of a progressive daily life, which necessitated the reformulation of two of its principal components: the social and ideological. Since everydayness consisted of fixed, lifeless "skeletal forms of existence" (*bytie*), everyday life had to generate its own transformation in such a way as to secure changes capable of eliminating barriers that had heretofore separated the everyday from the world of things, forms from content, subject from object. (It is interesting that in this early essay, Arbatov was approaching some of the considerations of Lukacsian subject/object identity, even though it is not likely that he was familiar with *History and Class Con-*

sciousness.) This self-generating process must accompany the continuing dissolution of class differences. The logic informing this proposal was clearly prompted by the recognition that since the everyday had been constituted as labor's opposite, social status was subsequently counterpoised to social dynamics, death against life. In bourgeois society, production was made to appear unrelated to existence and consumption and thus seen to have nothing to do with the way commodities were made. Once production was resituated at the heart of social existence to "form all aspects of human activity," the "static everyday life of consumption" would disappear, together with the "class technical divisions" signifying a capitalist society. But all this could "proceed only from the forms of material *byt*" (Arbatov, p. 121).

Historically, private ownership and the control of the means and forces of production induced the installation of a private and domestic everyday life. In fact, the idea of the private life was the sign of the bourgeois insistence on separating social life from productive activity. As a result, bourgeois life was characterized by the identity between private and "pure consumption" (Arbatov, p. 122)—saturated by the everydayness of the market. Arbatov was proposing here that in this environment, the bourgeoisie had managed to transform the thing into a commodity. This move echoed Tosaka Jun's observation a few years later that custom had become a stand-in for the commodity form. For Arbatov, the "capitalist street" was the site where things were displayed in stores, bought, and sold and where the "street origins" of prices were concealed from the "consciousness of the consumer." Hence the everyday life of the bourgeoisie became a sanctuary for private accumulation—"my things"—which referred to both the "material blessings" and "social-ideological categories."

Under this regime, the thing, now masked as a commodity, entered the "structure of everyday ceremony" to settle and colonize its "core"—propelled by the "cult of value, rarity, the antiquity of materials," all communicating the individual's socioeconomic status in an order of things determined by distinction. Even more important, the effect of masking things worked to obscure and repress its "utilitarian technical purpose" and its conditions of production. At this juncture in the narrative of everydayness, the "thing takes on a double meaning—both as material form and as ideological form" (p. 123). The subsequent alienation of consumption from production transformed the "thing relation" into a subjective, ideological, and taste-determined view of life to manufacture "style-ism" and "fashion." Both were possible only if the sites and conditions of production were suppressed and collective purpose was absent. Both conformed to the individual and his desire to discriminate, evaluate, and judge and thus adhere to the regime of aesthetic criteria that mandated standards of the "beautiful" or "ugly." Yet this move showed only the "aesthetic anarchy" driving bourgeois society, and the passivity of the "thing" in a society that never exceeded the goal of rearrangement. Things representing the fulfillment of the organism's physical capacity for labor, Arbatov observed, " as a force for social labor, as an instrument and as a co-worker," simply did not exist (p. 124).

Like so many in the industrializing world of the 1920s, Arbatov looked to the United States as the latest stage of capitalism in its most developed form and "Americanism" as the model that might yield a program for realigning the everyday with the world of production in the new socialist society. This admiration for "Americanism" referred to the organizational achievements of the large cities, not to the actual fusing of everyday life and production that have remained separate. Despite the continuing domination of the "financial bourgeoisie," this newest form of capitalism has reintroduced a "grandiose productive collectivization of society," and owing to the massive collectivization of labor, its cities have changed the role of the "technical intelligentsia." The "technical intelligentsia has now replaced its former everyday life with a new type, the everyday of enormous offices, department stores, factory laboratories, research institutes, and so on" (Arbatov, p. 125). Social space has been transformed from the "private apartment" into the "collective" realm linked to material production. Paradoxically, this transformation affected the technical intelligentsia, inasmuch as they found themselves separated from "private property relations" in order to acquire new values during the process of rationalization. In one sense, Arbatov was pointing to the dilemma of the petite bourgeoisie or white-collar classes who, in Germany as recorded by Kracauer and Japan as exemplified by Aono Suekichi, had advanced the process of rationalization even as they were stripped of their class entitlements. The importance of this shift in the Soviet Union was the way this class was able to transfer skills derived from the sphere of production to the domain of consumption, "from collective *byt* to private *byt*." A knowledge of things increasingly meant "rationalization" derived from the factory experience and was now becoming "active" in the formation of lived, material culture.

> The ability to pick up a cigarette case, to smoke a cigarette, to put on an overcoat, to wear a cap, to open the door, all these "trivialities" acquired their qualification, their not unimportant "culture," which finds its meaning in the maximization of economy and precision, in maximum cohesion with the things and its purpose. (p. 126)

In the texts of Kon Wajirō this observation on the importance of the most trivial gesture was transmuted into an occasion to envisage the formation of new subject positions based on the rationality of selecting objects of use value. Impressed by the necessity of organizing and controlling large-scale networks between things in the metropolitan city, Arbatov saw in this new, rationalized mode of cultural production the shaping of a new personality , indeed new subject positions empowered by their knowledge of "forms of gesticulation, movement, and activity." Physical culture, the infinite gestures and movements characterizing the "new image of the person," forced the evolution of the psychological disposition to become more "thinglike" in its associative structure. Describing the emergence of what might be called functionalism, in which class, steel, concrete, and artificial materials no longer needed to rely on ornamental masking but now "spoke for themselves" (Arbatov, p. 126), the mechanisms of the thing were now transparent, its content easily conformed to its form. But form "ceded its place to the primacy of a thing's functions" and the way it was constructed. With the "machine-ization of the thing," the thing of everyday consumption, "once static and dead," was now subordinated to the productive process. Hence new material forms of production and the necessity of reorganizing them, even more than the collectivization of society, installed a "monism of the thing," inasmuch as it determined the image of material forms of consumption that were now indistinct from it. Production methods infiltrated everyday life which, in turn, mediated them and thus "infused" itself into the productive process, making it more compatible with the conditions of labor. Soviet society was the first to reveal the fusion of these two tendencies, Arbatov believed, whose ultimate realization could come only with the full maturation of socialism.

While both sides of the fusion existed in "Americanism," capitalism was not in a position to realize it. According to Arbatov, the reason for this failure was the absence of the "dynamic laboring structure and its living force" in the relationship to the thing, which remained isolated, a thing in itself, the perfect figure of the commodity, "soulless." Capitalism's desire for nature was defeated by its "aversion" and "alienation." By the same token, the thing was cast outside nature, as if it had no connection, valuable only in itself, to lead a "fetishized" existence. His enthusiasm for new productive technologies that could resolve the question of social existence convinced him that it was possible to mend the rupture between the material energy of "society" and "nature," even though the process of rationalization had been directed to subject nature to its discipline. With electricity and radio, technical systems were increasingly implicated in work organized by human labor. "Here," Arbatov announced, "producing and consuming forms of energy are applied in the same way: nature in its pure form penetrates society and becomes *byt*" (Arbatov, p. 128). While neither Arbatov or Soviet society ever fulfilled the program of establishing an everyday life that was aligned with production and in which consumption conformed to the materiality and utility of the thing, when in fact the commodity form was banished, the effects were felt elsewhere. In Germany, Walter Benjamin rethought the possibilities inherent in a reunion of art and production in his famous "Author as Producer," and in Japan, Kon Wajirō's urban research led to a theory of subjectivity rooted in knowing how to consume things according to their utility. Above all else, Arbatov resolved the identification of everyday life with the worker, no longer the negative other of bourgeois life, until Michel DeCerteau broke up this union and transformed everydayness into a static and indefinite figure of social life characterized by the endless circulation of strategies and tactics, resembling the interminable game of musical chairs Adorno once observed of Karl Mannheim's conception of a sociology of knowledge.

In the capitalist West of Berlin, Siegfried Kracauer shared Arbatov's identification of the world of things but derived from Simmel his mode of actually experiencing them as the foci of everyday life and seeing them as the best way to grasp an always transitory modernity. In fact, Kracauer, more than Simmel, saw everydayness as an "exotic world," an "unknown place," comparable to the land of "primitives," especially the life of white-collar workers in the Germany of the 1920s and early 1930s. Everyday life was a virtual "terra incognito," as a later reflection described it in his *History: The Last Things Before the Last.*[37] Benjamin proposed that all of Kracauer's concerns with the discarded and forgotten detritus of modernity constituted a "confrontation with a piece of the everyday world, a built-up Here, a lived-out Now." Like his Japanese contemporary Tosaka Jun, who was celebrating the importance of journalism as a historical sign of everyday life neglected by academics, Kracauer's favored form were articles whose length seemed to match perfectly the new objects that had come to colonize everyday life. Even his book on the white-collar class, *Die Angestellten*, called attention to this form because it resembled an accumulation of short articles with timely and catchy titles.

If the site of Kracauer's account was the life of the white-collar class inhabiting the city of Berlin, it was because he, like Werner Sombart, believed that big cities were dominated less by industries than by "salaried employees and civil servants." For him, Berlin had become a "city with a pronounced employee culture," which meant one made by employees for employees, where they lived, worked, and played in the everydayness that wrote its history in these multiple activities. Rescuing this history was at the heart of Kracauer's conception of reportage, which did not mean the "reproduction of observed reality," even though he acknowledged that reportage, with its commitment to "concrete existence," had to be juxtaposed to the abstractions of idealism, despite its failure to "capture reality immediacy." Because observation has not "approach[ed] reality through a mediation," reality must always be a construction. Although reaching the reality of social existence depends on observation, observational reports do not necessarily account for what is happening. For Kracauer, the real resembled a "mosaic" pieced together from "single observations" intensified by an understanding of their meaning. "Reportage photographs life; such a mosaic should be its image" (A, p. 9; SM, p. 32).

But Kracauer was committed to this form, not as a reporter or even as an "orthodox Marxist" devoted to an analysis driven by a dialectical desire to "unmask," but, rather, according to Benjamin, as a "rag picker" sifting through the residues of modern life for fragments that might tell of "the small catastrophes that make up everyday life." The form of the feuilleton narrated the scraps that cluttered everyday life, constantly changing novelties collected into collages of the snapshots Simmel privileged as the object of analysis. "The place which an epoch occupies in the historical process is determined more forcefully in the analysis of its insignificant superficial manifestations than from the judgments of the epoch itself" (MO, p. 109). Japanese thinkers as different as the native ethnologist Yanagita Kunio and the Marxist philosopher Tosaka agreed similarly that what constituted everyday life were the innumerable objects, which they called custom, derived from the past and now a modern present. For them, the encounter between the old and the new determined the historicity of everyday life far more precisely than did the larger claims of political and economic modernization. For Kracauer, there was the pursuit to reclaim from the modern new an everydayness "whose claim to be acknowledged . . . has not yet been recognized.[38] Like a newspaper article, the scraps revealed the forms of a hidden existence of history that the superficial phenomena of everyday life suppressed in the interest of fashion and novelty.

If Kracauer turned to the surface phenomena, the trivia of everyday life cropping up everywhere, this choice was prompted by a strategy of looking beyond what was immediately given. This return to the material forms through which their existence was negotiated meant extracting from a meaningless and not always knowable objective world only the promise of waiting in a state of "hesitant openness." Like Simmel, Kracauer was rarely optimistic about the human ability to understand the spectacle of the objective world and to derive a lasting and stable meaning from it. In his essay "Those Who Wait," like the books *Die Detektive Roman* and *Die Angestellten*, he described this objective world as one offering neither shelter or meaning but only "homelessness," a domain dominated by indifferent conventions that have acquired the appearance of a "second nature."[39] "One waits, and one's waiting is a *hesitant openness* . . . difficult to explain. . . . One ought to think primarily of those people who have tarried and still do tarry in front of closed doors; and who thus, when they take it upon themselves to wait, are people who are waiting here and now" (*MO*, p. 138). Even the hotel lobby, the space that dominates his essay on the detective novel, promotes a "togetherness that has no meaning." The people who gather there "become detached from everyday life," but the detachment does not result in the reconstitution of a community, displacing "people from the unreality of the daily hustle and bustle to a place they . . . encounter the void" (*MO*, p. 176).

Kracauer was pointing to the urban middle classes who have "eluded the profession of a particular faith," who fail to congregate into a community of meaning, but who have acquired sufficient wealth and cultural capital "to live with an alert sense of their time" (p. 129). (I should point out that Kracauer saw the religious community as a unified and meaningful form. "Through the edification of the congregation, the community is always reconstructing itself, and this elevation above the everyday prevents the everyday from going under" was a sentiment that undoubtedly represented a return to Max Weber.) This urban middle and professional class spend most of their days in loneliness—forgetting in the "hustle" and "bustle" of everyday life their "inner being." They suffer from a "profound sadness," a metaphysical malaise stemming from the absence of "meaning in the world," a "purposiveness without purpose." Existing in empty space, they are bonded "companions of misfortune" (p. 177). An everyday world devoid of meaning, colonized by commodities, "haphazardly" animating trivial conversations "aimed at utterly insignificant objects so that one might encounter oneself in their exteriority" (p. 181), calls forth the "mass ornament," "abstract," "ambiguous," dominated by the "Ratio of the capitalist economic system" which "is not reason itself but a murky reason" (pp. 83, 81). Elsewhere, he proclaimed that the human subject was "thrown out into the cold infinity of empty space and time."[40]

Although Kracauer saw the everyday world as empty, he was nevertheless determined to return to the immediacy of concrete experience, especially those "surface-level expressions" which, "by virtue of their unconscious nature, provide unmediated access to the fundamental substance of the state of things" (MO, p. 75). A formal, empirical sociology was no longer adequate to the task, as Simmel had already argued, because the world was no longer filled with recognizable meaning, as it was now occupied by chaos, individual shards of now absent, meaningful coherence. It is important to remember that Kracauer, like Simmel and other social theorists confronting the spectacle of modernity, posited the prior existence of a unified, coherent world to explain the fragmentary nature of contemporary experience. As a strategy, this echoed Tönnies's presumption of a Gemeinschaft that existed before the establishment of a Gesellschaft. But it is hard not to conclude that this prior imaginary was produced after the fact and that the supposed unity was a way of justifying and making meaningful an analysis that concentrated on the appearance of an immediately given but fragmented experience. Abstract, formal categories applied to ordering immediate reality could work only in an "epoch filled with meaning."[41] What the present required instead was a phenomenology devoted to determining "intentional existence and events." "Knowledge of the state of things," Kracauer wrote, "depends on the interpretation of the surface level expressions. The fundamental absence of an epoch and its unheeded impulses illuminate each other reciprocally" (*MO*, p. 75). In an appeal to a revised Marxism capable of accounting for "surface expressions," the experiential and the superficiality of everyday life, he proposed to Ernst Bloch that "the notion of totality should not blind one to the instances of superficial life. To start from the substantive and superficial seems to me not to be banished from a genuine revolutionary theory."[42]

Much as Simmel and Benjamin had done, Kracauer's apparent return to the concrete immediacy of everyday life concentrated on the fragments, the leavings of life, aphorisms assigned to supply philosophical meaning. Kracauer's return to the real of everyday life, its materiality, was announced in *The Detective Novel* (1922–1925), which was an instance of the superficial and insignificant and was called to stand in as the microcosm for the macrocosmic everyday world. But it was in his collection of short essays, *The Mass Ornament* (1927), and his pioneering book on the white-collar class, *Die Angestellten* (1930), that he demonstrated his approach to concrete immediacy and his ability to read beneath the surface of everyday life for a history that had been banished. Here, Kracauer's purpose was to demythologize, calling attention to Weber's earlier recognition of a demystifying process marking Western history, and a strategy that promised to disclose how mythology continued to adorn and conceal reason like an ornament (*MO*, pp. 80–81).

The world portrayed in these essays is mediated by American material culture, a historical experience characterizing Japan, France, and Italy, what Kracauer referred to as a cultural topography produced by "American distraction factories" (*MO*, pp. 75–76). The prototype of this "Americanization" was the Tiller Girls, whose machinelike precision resembled the assembly line. "The hands in the factory," he observed, "correspond to the legs of the Tiller Girls" (p. 79). Contrasted with ballet, which still retained its historical connection to an erotic life that "both gave rise to them and determined their traits," the mass movements of the Tiller Girls demonstrated only "mathematics" (p. 76) and "took place in a vacuum; they are a linear system that no longer has any erotic meaning" and in which the ornament becomes an end in itself. Timeless, historyless, the performance is emptied of substantial content (p. 77). For Kracauer, the mass ornament was the "aesthetic reflex of the rationality pursued by the capitalist mode of production" (pp. 78–79). It is a "mythological cult" cloaked in abstraction. When the mass ornament, like the Tiller Girls, is compared with the "concrete immediacy of other material presentations," its appeal to reason is seen as an "illusion" (p. 83). Reason has failed to penetrate the mass ornament, whose "patterns," like the commodity, remain "mute." The ratio that has given it life has also eliminated all life from the figures constituting it, too weak to find humans in it or even history or knowledge. Reason is thus closed off from the "capitalist Ratio" to produce a "rational and empty form of the cult, devoid of an specific meaning" (p. 84).

The mass ornament resembles most "aerial photographs of landscapes and cities" because it never emerges from their interiors and a given set of conditions but, rather, looms above them (p. 77). Like photography, it is detached from its bearers and remains always in the present. Photography shares this defect with historicism inasmuch as both presume to present a continuum—spatial in the former, temporal in the latter. The importance of this coupling is how each seeks to grasp what is given as a spatial or temporal continuum but cannot discern what is truly significant. Kracauer reserved the function of designating the significant for memory, which is both fragmentary and temporally discontinuous but whose images manage to embrace a truth. The images storing traits that consciousness recalls are related to what has been considered true. For this reason, these images are distinguished from all other memory—images because they preserve only those elements that "touch on" what has been "recognizably true." Accordingly, memory preserves the last image—which is the most unforgettable one.

Kracauer was convinced that this last image of, say, a person was his or her "actual history." Neither photography nor history could supply such images linked to truth. A history produced by a fragment is not a narrative that fills out the temporal continuum from beginning to end or the space of a photo; it is a "monogram"—a condensation into meaningful figures. Photography, and received conventions of historical practice, succeeds only to bury the actual history of a person, "as if under a layer of snow" (*MO*, p. 51). For the specific history to glimmer through the layer of snow, the surface coherence presented by the photograph "must be destroyed" (p. 52). Kracauer compared the artwork, which he saw as a construction whose meaning assumes a spatial appearance, with the photograph in which the spatial representation of an object is all the meaning it emits. In both photography and historicism, the appeal to verisimilitude actually evacuates meaning. Unlike the operation of memory, the photograph effaces the truth content of the original left behind in a forgotten history. "It captures only the residuum that history has discharged," "sediments settled from the monogram." As a result, photography is bound to time, like fashion, principally because it has only a momentary significance, "like a human garb," "transparent when modern and abandoned when old" (p. 55). Nothing says more about history than what was once fashionable, even though its newness disavowed the historical. In the photograph, representation manages to snare only contexts and images when the "liberated consciousness" that once envisaged them has departed. But now it frames only "orders of existence" that have faded "without wanting to admit" the passage of time and intention. What such photographs seek to banish is the sign of the fear of death itself, its recollection (which always accompanies memory images), and ultimately history. In the illustrated magazines of his time, everyday life was made into a "photographical present," and this photographical present became "eternalized." Far from being an escape from death and history, it is a sign of surrender to it.

In Kracauer's conception of everyday life, this eternalized present—undoubtedly inspired by Simmel—which appears only to have banished death and history in the countless "distractions" offered by capitalism in great cities like Berlin, was lived by a new middle class that he identified in his 1930 book, *Die Angestellten*, as the white-collar worker. Simultaneously but coincidentally, the Japanese literary critic and writer Aono Suekichi wrote a book on Japan's middle class, entitled *Sararīman kyōfu jidai* (The period of middle-class panic), a year later, which, as Kracauer did, analyzed the psychological state of the new middle classes in Japan's cities that had succumbed to the consumption of the new commodities and could no longer fulfill their expectations.

Kracauer's book combined journalistic reportage and urban ethnography, observing and interviewing, to produce a series of snapshot studies of this class at work and play—the modes of experiencing the reality of white-collar existence in the large cities. These white-collar workers, like their Japanese counterpart, were squeezed between industrial labor and big business, composed of an older stratum derived from a precapitalist economy and a newer one based on salaried employees in commerce, bureaucracy, and the newer service industries. What seemed to attract Kracauer was their stubborn desire for identification as an estate or status grouping (*stand*) and their disavowal of proletarianization. Hence, they insisted on upholding an image of social distance from industrial workers and presuming social and cultural superiority over them, even though they were no better off economically. The continuing rationalization of the German economy contributed to the workers' experience of alienation, atomization, and anomie. Contrasted with industrial workers, who had the prospect of being informed of meaning by "vulgar Marxist concepts," white-collar workers were "intellectually homeless." They had been evicted from the "house of bourgeois ideas and feelings in which they previously lived," owing to collapsed foundations brought on by economic development. "A vanished bourgeois way of life haunts them" (SM, pp. 82, 88; A, pp. 76, 85). They live in a present with no doctrine to guide them. Kracauer charted the path that white-collar workers pursued in this landscape of meaninglessness—especially those activities that promised instant "distraction" and the allure of "objects" that glittered. People spent so much time in bars and cafes because life at home was so miserable and "they want[ed] to experience excitement."

Life at home encompassed the everyday as well as the "residential" life, as represented by advertisements in magazines for white-collar employees. The inventory of distraction included "Kohinoor pencils," hemorrhoids, hair loss, beds, crepe soles, white teeth, rejuvenation treatments, coffee consumption habits, Dictaphones, writer's cramp, trembling in the presence of others, and quality pianos on weekly installment plans. "Girls come mostly from modest circumstances and get seduced by the glamour." Serious conversation was dismissed as a distraction from the "surroundings they would like to enjoy." Where these workers throng together, as in cities like Berlin, they organize their own "shelters," giant club houses in which "one can feel the wide world for little money" (A, p. 85; SM, p. 88). These shelters "still the hunger of big city dwellers for glamour and distraction." Even contemporary film, Kracauer observed first in the earlier essays like "The Little Shop Girls Go to the Movies" and "Contemporary Films and Its Audience," abolishes the existing state of things by failing to examine either its excesses or its basic foundations. Illustrated newspaper and magazines functioned similarly to numb people with the "pseudo glamour of counterfeit social heights." But recurring pictorial motifs sent substantive matters into a state of "pictureless amnesia," bracketing existence itself. "The flight of the image," he declared, "is the flight from revolution and death" (A, p. 93; SM, p. 94). In the same way, sports merely symptomized "repression on a grand scale," since they failed to reform social relations but only depoliticized them.

　　Kracauer's examination of everyday life lived and experienced by the white-collar class was aimed at showing the persistence of false consciousness and how a group's apparently real interests were constantly being thwarted and displaced in distractions. While his own return to the concrete of everyday life signaled a move away from the consolations of religion—which, like Simmel and even Lukacs and Benjamin, Weber identified with the non-everyday—its main purpose was to report on received experience and unmask it for some vague goal of politicizing his own class, the intelligentsia (MO, p. 94). But Kracauer's return to the concrete present of everydayness did as much to affirm its eternality as it did to recall a history it has effaced. The examination of the white-collar class described the consequences of "ratio-induced disintegration." Once emptied of all substantive content, these classes were no longer subject to anything other than "the binding neutrality of

contentless thought" (pp. 113, 93). The economic and social system took refuge in the "muteness of such thinking." In the end,
Kracauer was convinced that there was still the promise of one
who "waits" but who has shifted focus from a "theoretical self to
the self of the entire human being" and who, leaving an unreal
world, has embraced one of reality and its domain, which for Kracauer was an indeterminate world of "hesitant openness" (p. 139).
But history was also made to wait, as if in some momentary illumination it would reveal itself and the course that had to be taken.
In this way, "hesitant openness" could be read as a description of
Kracauer's position between the eternalizing present of Simmel's
and Lukacs's different programs to break out of the iron cage of
reification and achieve the identity of subject/object. But not quite.

It was Walter Benjamin who identified the purpose of Kracauer's *Die Angestellten* as explaining a "section of everyday life,
an inhabited Here and lived Now" (*SM*, p. 111). But seizing hold
of this everydayness required understanding the experience lived
by the "salariat." Benjamin was swayed that no other class in the
present day thought and felt more alienated from the "concrete
reality of its everyday existence" (p. 110). Because this class stood
in a "far more indirect relation to the productive process," it found
itself more directly implicated in the "interpersonal relations"
mediated by large-scale organizations that "reified" rather than
humanized personal relations. For that reason, Kracauer was com-
pelled to construct a critique of unionism. Through interviews and
observation at the labor court, he discovered that the union's
pledge to represent the white-collar worker produced the reverse
results. Instead of liberating employees from ideological fetters, it
only reinforced their hold. "If . . . trade unions advocate a rational
ordering of economic life that imparts some comprehensible
meaning to the individual's activity, . . . they seek to provide consciousness with contents that do not alter its relationship to mech-
anized work." These contents "evaporate" once they are secured
as possessions, since they are used just to "fill people out or elevate them above their everyday existence." The purpose is to
remove the drawbacks of mechanization by means of spiritual pal-
liatives "administered like medicines." But this peddling of nos-

trums is itself a sign of the reification they are trying to eliminate. "It is sustained," Kracauer added, "by the notion that such contents represent ready-made facts to be delivered" (A, pp. 104–105; SM, p. 102). Cultural goods, as he named them, like conceptions of community—taken from the "scraps of the bourgeois kitchen" and now offered at cut-rate prices—express not the collectivity of like-minded people but only the will to it, revealing solely an operation that presumes to identify the meaning of the collectivity it is supposed to embody but really avoids the more difficult task of producing a knowledge capable of founding and binding a community. Kracauer proposed that the individual who confronts death alone is never "submerged" in the collectivity defining its ultimate purpose but, rather, finds self-formation through the knowledge from which the community may also emerge. "What matters," he concluded, "is not that institutions are changed, what matters is that human individuals change institutions" (A, p. 109; SM, p. 106).

It was this disavowal of death that Kracauer and others recognized in everyday life as a lived experience and a history (which he and others called *historicism*) that "records the temporal succession of events" whose linkage does not contain the transparency of history that partly explains Martin Heidegger's repositioning of death as the enabling condition for reconceptualizing history into repetition and everyday life into authentic existence. If Heidegger saw history as simply a temporal order that fails to "preserve" the history that consciousness reads out of the succession of events, his own solution to the problem never went beyond envisioning a new role for the memory image in a world in which both historicism and photography missed the opportunity of presenting the significant. While *Being and Time* (1926) was, among many things, a powerful rethinking of the whole question of existence and was ultimately linked to considerations of modernity and everyday life, its reconceptualization of history in light of an inauthentic everyday existence raised a challenge that only Walter Benjamin seemed willing to assume.[43]

What I mean is that Heidegger's identification of history as it was commonly understood and its connection to an inauthentic everyday resulted in a rethinking of both and their mode of relating to which, it seems to me, Benjamin's program for historical materialism tried to provide an alternative. I am suggesting that Heidegger's rearticulation of the problem of existence and time ultimately problematized the relationship between everydayness and history so as to challenge all subsequent attempts to think the history of the present. Unlike Kracauer, who appealed to the possibility of another kind of history without seeing through a program, Benjamin started with history, that is, prehistory, and worked toward a conception of historical construction that, despite its reliance on repetition, stood in marked contrast to Heidegger's notion of historicality. The difference turned on how each subsequently envisaged everyday life and historical temporality.

More than any thinker in the interwar period, Heidegger tackled the status of everydayness (*Alltagslichkeit*) and Being's fall into the world of "They" (*das Man*). Although it was Edmund Husserl, according to Kracauer, who supplied the philosophy for the newly discovered everyday, which he named the *social life world*, it was Heidegger who in many ways explicitly defined the everyday in modernity, even though he reduced it to its primordial dimensions and reconfigured its understanding for all subsequent discussions. But it would be wrong to separate this reconfiguration from contemporary discussions like those of Simmel, Weber, and Lukacs, whose writings resonate in Heidegger's great text and whose formulations on everydayness and history are echoed in the work of Kracauer, Benjamin, and Marcuse.

It was Heidegger's purpose to relocate Being's existence in a structure of temporality different from ordinary everyday life and its historiography, which "endeavors to alienate Dasein from its authentic historicality" (*BT*, p. 448). This move required constructing what he called an "authentic historiology" that might deprive "today" of its character as "present," which "becomes a way of painfully detaching oneself from the falling publicness of 'today'" (p. 449). It is plain, he proposed, that Being's "inauthentic historicality" is rooted in "everydayness" and that an authentic historicality must be rediscovered in "Dasein's primordial temporality" (pp. 428, 429). Heidegger was convinced, of course, that the

authentic temporality deriving from Being's primordiality originated in the anticipation of death. "Being free for death" gives
Dasein its goal and "pushes its existence into finitude" (p. 435).
This recognition of death's anticipation and thus the finitude of
existence reveal Being's "primordial historicizing," which itself is
rooted in an "authentic resoluteness" against the inconstancies of
distraction and opens the way to the "moment of vision of antici-
pating repetition" that will deprive the "today" of its character as
"present" (p. 442). (The Japanese philosopher Tosaka Jun, as we
will see, tried to retain this identity between the today and the present in order to grasp the moment of historicity it signified.) The
moment weans one from all the conventionalities associated with
the "They" (pp. 443–444).

Heidegger saw authenticity (*Eigentlichkeit*) as an act of appro-
priating one's own, which meant claiming and thus choosing one's
fate in the face of one's own death. Authentic history referred to
a fateful repetition of "possibilities," as opposed to the distractions,
disconnectedness, and dispersions lost in the world of the They (p.
442). In this world of the They, notoriously reminiscent of the one
Kracauer and Simmel had already described—even though Heidegger did not give it sociological specificity—choice is avoided
and thus fails to repeat what has once been, retaining only the
"actual" that remains as a residue, the "leavings" and the "information present at hand." Once lost in making present "today," the
past is understood only in terms of the present. Here, Heidegger
dismissed the same kind of historicism that Kracauer had already
discredited, which tried only to fill out the temporal succession,
as well as Benjamin's rejection of a historical practice that aspired
to "universal history" and the deadening evolutionary trajectory
toward the "same." In Heidegger's reformulation, the inauthentic
history inscribed in the everyday was weighted with the legacy of
the "past" which had "become unrecognizable" as it sought to realize the modern (p. 444). For Heidegger, the "modern" was everyday life as it was being lived by the They. It is important to emphasize that everydayness was refigured into the place of negativity,
which later historians of *Alltagsgeschicte* tried to undo and recode
as the site of positive experience.

The logic of *Being and Time* demanded primordial identification, which meant returning to the base world of Being—its everydayness (*BT*, p. 151). But the everydayness that is immediately given
is the habitus of an "I" that has lost itself. Hence, to answer the
"who" of Dasein, Heidegger believed it was necessary to analyze
Being in the environment "closest to us" and to the Others of the
world it encounters. It is in this world that Dasein's capacity to know
itself is led astray and unhappily obstructs the various possibilities
available to Being (p. 163). Being thus takes refuge in substitutes,
falling into a world of averageness and mediocrity that conceals
from Being the possibilities it itself possesses. In this immediate
environment, the "close at hand," "Dasein's everyday possibilities
of Being are taken for others to dispose of but any other can represent them." Heidegger's "who" of Being is simply the "neuter" of
the "They," since it is neither that one nor itself; in fact, it is not
even the "sum of all." The environment that establishes the condition of a " dictatorship" of the "They" and is closest at hand is what
Heidegger called a "public environment" (p. 164). By using public
transportation and information services such as the newspapers,
every other is like the next. This collective "They" signals an averaging and leveling down of Being's possibilities that seeks to destroy
differences, as it is nothing definite but the Being of everydayness.
Everyday life is this publicness (*Offentlichkeit*) which contrives to
obscure everything, especially the way in which the world is inter-
preted, that is, what, at bottom, is "familiar" and "accessible" to all.

There is no answerability in this environment, no exercise of
responsibility or accountability because the location of enunciation is always indefinite. It is always the "They" who make pronouncements, which means only that "it was no one." Adorno later
linked this conception of flattening to exchange itself, since it
resembles the "leveling" that the "exchanger" usually experiences
"through his inevitable reduction to the equivalence form;" that
is, the critique of political economy understanding exchange value
in terms of the social work—time that is on the average spent.[44]
In this inauthentic everyday world, everyone is the other, as interchangeable as hands on an assembly line, and no one is himself.
Thus the self is "disburdened" by the They, and Being, failing to

"stand by oneself" slips helplessly and unhappily into inauthenticity (*BT*, p. 166). Heidegger calls this state of slipping the "they-self," which he believed prevents the self from exercising the courage of anxiety in the face of death (p. 298). The everyday world of the "They" offers the refuge of escape from death, and the timeless succession of events offers the appearance of a continuous existence and the illusion that death happens to others. The sign of this falling is temptation, tranquillity, and alienation (pp. 298, 210–224).

If Heidegger's formulation of everydayness obscured the primordiality of Being's true existence so as to resemble a thick ideological screen that has prevented people from recognizing their true interest, as Lukacs had already proposed, it also carefully avoided the specificity of social form. Yet its frequent appeals to "idle talk," "chatter," "alienation," "averageness," and the like identified it with a world already being lived and experienced in the modern, mass societies of the great metropolitan centers. The everyday world of inauthenticity he saw as a fallen or degraded state was plainly the "potentiality for Being in the world," and the realization of authentic existence was not something floating above everydayness but represented only a "modified way in which everydayness is seized upon." In a certain sense, this purpose was shared by Walter Benjamin, who in his later works increasingly turned away from religion for the concreteness offered by everyday life, in order to redeem it from the degraded state to which Heidegger had committed it and to find the resoluteness needed to "modify" it. It was, in fact, this return to the concrete of what was immediately given as a historical formation rather than the flight to primordial identification, a conception of the construction of life akin to political action rather than the absence of a theory of repetition, that accounts for the real difference between Benjamin and Heidegger and their political positions. Benjamin was as socially specific and sensitive to historical forms in his writings as Heidegger was indefinite and indeterminate. But both, we should recall, tried to reconceptualize what they understood as historicism in order to rescue from surface routine the possibility offered by a buried past. The present and its everyday would be the place to perform what

Benjamin termed a "blasting operation." As socially unspecific Heidegger was, Benjamin's celebration of concreteness was immersed in all the recognizable forms of modernity and the city. In an early work, he appealed to a knowledge consisting of multiple expressions grounded in "the concrete totality of experience, that is, existence."[45]

Almost at the same time, the Japanese philosopher Tosaka Jun was announcing that thought itself was becoming "quotidianized" as the sign of a concreteness produced by everyday life—its historical mark—to counter the claims of philosophical abstraction promoting a concept of reality (*genjitsu*) which moved considerations from the immediate and performative present to the past. Tosaka, like Benjamin, later discarded this conception of "reality" as simply false concreteness—as a form of appearance—in order to emphasize the concrete present and the idea of "actuality."

It is important to point out that the apparent kinship and difference between Heidegger and Benjamin became dramatically apparent in their conceptions of time and historical temporality. The time that Heidegger named as vulgar and inauthentic, Benjamin, as we shall see, qualified as progressive. Both, however, envisaged in time a succession and accumulation of presents and thus saw modernity as the temporality called the "new" and the end of the present. The idea of an end of the present made possible a full possession of time. Heidegger, we must recall, had argued that it was necessary to think time after recognizing Dasein's finitude, after its being "thrown," to become a being for death. Even if Being now had no foundation, it was still incessantly "projecting" before itself. It was thus Dasein's finitude, its itinerary in time, that permitted the possibility of an authentic and inauthentic temporality.

Inauthentic time was steeped in inauthentic understanding that did not recognize Being's finitude and so diverted Dasein as being for death. According to Heidegger, this diversion from true destiny is accomplished through a triple inauthenticity of future, present, and past: "waiting for" and the "ecstasy" that anticipates the next moment that will succeed and take the place of the preceding; the "now" that presupposes the constancy and permanence

of the present, its eternity; and the "memory" of the past that sup-
poses that each present moment is deposited and thus stored up
in memory. By the same measure, authentic temporality knows
only the "ecstasy" of Dasein in time, of being's "thrown-ness"—
projected to go out and meet itself. To become oneself for authentic existence is to recapture Dasein's being thrown into the world
and its recognition that time has already been given "behind itself."
Thus there is a corresponding triple ecstasy—"anticipation," the
"instant," and the "repetition." A genuinely authentic history in
this scheme is possible only with this understanding of time, as
opposed to its reverse which is posited on a continual succession,
representing only the artificiality of clock time, or a preoccupation
with the "new," details and the inessential. Here Heidegger and
Benjamin rejected the received historicist traditions of historiography, for two different reasons. If Benjamin saw in the historicist
conception of continuous progress a fiction that obeyed the logic
of the commodity in its commitment to a causal scheme in which
one event is followed and replaced another—like the new that was
always being replaced and the old that was instantly disappearing—Heidegger accused it of diverting Being from its true vocation by giving it the illusion of immortality. For Heidegger, history was produced by the injunctions of "futural" destiny, and its
condition therefore required de-actualizing the false today, the
everydayness of the "They," an inauthentic present, in order to
realize the possibility of a future that is always repeated.

Benjamin, as we shall see, would agree on the necessity of
deconstructing the present in order to identify the possibilities
deposited from the past. He disagreed with Heidegger, however,
in his rejection of the demands of the future—destiny—and the
need to make a resolute choice that would result in a repetition
of the past, repeating the possibilities offered by Dasein, its community, or its "most proper past." The resolute response that would
result in a saving jump (not Benjamin's "Tiger's leap") to a future
in the distance also obscured and undermined the potential of the
present to provide possibilities that would secure a different future.
In Benjamin's thinking, the order was reversed. Both historicism
with its figuration of the commodity form in narrative and its insis-

tence on causal succession events and Heidegger's call for a repetitive history of the archaic in a present demanded by the future
were rejected for a "redemptive" or "messianic" historiography that
posited the present's discontinuity from the claims of progress and
its difference from a completed and now discarded past. The problem was not to hear and understand the appeal of the future voic-
ing destiny's injunction but, rather, to respond to the past's expectation that has waited to be reactivated in the present. That is, the
problem was not to make a sudden leap worthy of a time to come
that signified the repetition of the "possible having been" but,
rather, to recapture the impossible, to pay one's debt to what was
never possible and was always prevented.[46] For Benjamin, the present offered an opportunity for actualizing not the "having been"
as such but the forgotten. In this modality, history was powered
not by the yet to come—which merely replaced what had already
occurred, like the commodity that appears and disappears with the
ever-new—but by the "actualization" of the past, because the present now made available the moment to articulate the "critical
point" of what was necessary to consider.

As I have already suggested, this was a politicization of history,
investing it with a political vocation that both historicism and Heidegger's repetitive "historicality" tried to avoid in the fateful years
before World War II. According to Benjamin:

> What distinguishes the images from "essences" of phenomenol-
> ogy is historically their mark. [Heidegger searches in vain to save
> history for phenomenology abstractly, with the idea of "histori-
> cality."] These must be completely distinguished from the cate-
> gories of the "spiritual sciences," those called habitus, style, etc.
> The historical mark of images does not solely indicate that they
> belong to a determinate time, it especially indicates that they have
> achieved only a legibility in a determinate time. And this fact
> manages to achieve for legibility a critical point determined from
> the movement which is interior to it. Each present is determined
> by that which is synchronic with it: each Now is the now of a
> determined knowability. In it, truth is weighed down with time
> until it explodes. [This explosion, and nothing other, is the death

of intention which coincides with the birth of authentic historical images.] It is not that the past that projects its light on the
present or that the present projects its light on the past; rather it
is that image is what has been [*das Gewesene*] entered into a con-
stellation with the now in a flash of lightning. In other terms the
image is the dialectic at a stop. Because now the relation of the
present to the past is purely a temporal relation, the relation of
another time with the Now is dialectical: not of temporal nature
but of a figurative one. Only dialectical images are authentic historic images, that is to say, nonarchaic images. . . . The image in
the now of knowability carries to a higher degree the mark of the
critical moment . . . which is the foundation of all reading.[47]

If Heidegger is too abstract, uninterested in analyzing social
forms or concrete historical existence, Benjamin is no more interested in interrogating the conditions of social existence and promoting the promise of social history. But unlike Heidegger, Benjamin was intensely involved in exposing material details appropriate
to specific epochs. Where the Heideggerian "historicity" foundered
was in its confusion of "essences" and "historical images." The present has no essence but only an image, as we have seen, a physiognomy, a "face" that has neither being nor essence. It is in a state of
sleep waiting to be awakened. The sleeping state is not an ancient
present now become a past but a past already forgotten that waits
for a new present to summon it from its dormant state.

For Benjamin, under these circumstances, time is not linear,
successive, or even repetitive, even though there is more than a hint
of it in the way the relationship between present and past is structured, but more properly "intertwined," eliciting the figure of the
"arabesque." By displacing the three moments of past, present, and
future and intermingling them so as to form a strange topography
of twists and turns, "they weave an inextricable arabesque." Because
it is not solely the present, past, and future of empty time that constantly mingle with one another but also the true, lived time of the
present, the time present to consciousness forms a complex weave
of warp and woof. The first row of "empty time" is interwoven with
a second row that forms the present, past, and future of "full time,"

a "pure time, that superimposes itself on the first to continuously produce a doubling."[48] Hence, the arabesques are the curves of lines, spins, spirals, or scrolling that double back to create a vast labyrinth that blurs the beginning and the end, the entrance and the exit of time. For Benjamin, it was the everyday of the present that housed this labyrinth of time and provided the place in which to enact the synchronic drama in which past, present, and future are interwoven in an endless tapestry of temporality.

Benjamin's goal was to rethink everyday life as part of a larger program aimed at imagining a new approach to historical materialism, since the older one had clearly bypassed its place in modern society. "The dialectical representation of history," he wrote when commenting on Engels,

> is paid for by renouncing the contemplativeness which characterizes historicism. The historical materialist must abandon the epic element in history; for him history becomes the object of a construct [*Konstruktion*] which is not located in empty time but is constituted in a specific epoch. . . . The historical materialist explodes the epoch out of its reified historical continuity, and thereby lifts life out of this epoch. . . . Historicism presents the eternal image of the past; historical materialism presents a given experience with the past, an experience which stands unique.[49]

Benjamin envisioned a different kind of temporality for his materialist history and appealed to such strategies as "dialectics at a standstill," "messianic cessation," and "dialectical image" as a way of getting out of conventional theories of progress represented by the received historicist historiography in order to contemplate the concrete in a nonhistoricist setting. The present must be relieved from its identification with the eternal past and be nourished by the now. In this regard, Benjamin's everydayness contrasts with Kracauer's sense of presentness, which remained undifferentiated from the now, its point always vanishing, to be succeeded by the ever-new. In Kracauer's writings, the search for the transformation in the city inevitably reaffirms the present which, like the commodity, appears to be unhistorical. The present is empty time filled

not with history, as it should be, but with fortuitous, empty space—
the streets. Everyday life is eternalizing, deserted, much like
DeCerteau's later refiguration of the practice of daily life.

For Benjamin, there is a constant clash between the ever-new,
fashion, and novelty and the recently outmoded that continues to
exist in a modernity characterized by its ceaselessly produced newness. In "Central Park," he put it in the following way: "Dialectic
of commodity production: the newness of the product acquires (as
a stimulus of demand) a hitherto unheard-of-significance; the ever-
always-the-same appears palpably in mass-production for the first
time."[50] But as he observed about Baudelaire, the new never indicates a contribution to progress but only what has already disappeared. Thus modernity, especially everyday existence and experience, becomes the site where the past is always situated in the
present and where differing forms of historical consciousness constantly commingle and interact. That is, modernity is not only a
distinct form of experience stemming from new social practices
but also a "decisive mutation of historical experiences," which
accordingly "produce a range of possible temporalizations" and
the certainty for "competition or struggle" between them in everyday life.[51] This is what Tosaka identified as the moment when a
"convention" would be replaced by newer ones. These competing
temporalizations refer to the coexistence of differing moments,
almost a layering of todays. The past, implanted in an ongoing
present—identified by Baudelaire, according to Benjamin, as the
"transitory," the "fugitive," and the "contingent"—prefigures the
permanence of unevenness that capitalism made as a condition of
its continued expansion in political economy but refigured in cultural forms.

While this observation was worked out after World War II by
Henri Lefebvre, who declared it to be a characteristic of everyday
life, it was already implicit in Benjamin's recognition of competing historical temporalizations, the past in the present and Ernst
Bloch's more explicit identification of "nonsynchronous contem-
poraneities," not to mention a number of Japanese thinkers
obsessed with the experience of their own modernity. In *Pas-
sagenwerk*, Benjamin called the nineteenth century a "space of

time" (*Zeitraum*), which recalled "the dream of time" (*Zeit Traum*) and thereby revealed where the struggle between competing temporalizations was carried out (*Passages*, p. 406). This idea of the "space of time" draws attention to Tosaka Jun's remarkable conceptualization of everydayness into space (*nichijosei no kukan*) which structured its temporality into accumulative layers that could be disturbed only by exploring the possibilities they offer or make accessible at a given moment. Moreover, this recognition of unevenness signified not just the concurrence of different cycles in the everyday, as Lefebvre proposed, but also produced those inflections of specific cultures differentiating the historical experience of modernity to supply, as Japan and other societies showed, coeval, not alternative, modernities that challenged the universalizing and homogenizing claims of the Western example.

For Benjamin, the commodity form was at the heart of everyday life. Both its capacity to conceal (and thus forget) its enabling conditions of production and its talent for interpellating consumers (what he called its power of "empathy") revealed its role in making the everyday the space of differing historical temporalizations at the same time as it made it the place for producing again the redemptive power associated with tradition—constructing history—in the time of modernity. That is, the commodity form that produced the ever-new in the ever-same—the "atrophying of experience"[52]—yielded the difference necessary to transform empty, homogeneous time with a now-time promising new possibilities.

The "commodity," which Marx described as a "mysterious thing," became the mysterious everyday life. "All the magic and necromancy that surround the products of labor, as long as they take the form of the commodities, vanishes heretofore, as soon as we come to other forms of production." Marx was convinced, as was Benjamin, that religion was only a "reflex of the world," and Christianity with its "cults of abstraction" was the most effective device in reducing social relations as commodities and values and in homogenizing "human labor." This religion would "vanish" only "when the practical relations of everyday life offer to man none but perfectly intelligible and reasonable relations."[53] Marx deciphered these social hieroglyphics in terms of the social character of the labor that produced them, and thus questioned the very history they forgot. To Benjamin, however—following the lead of the surrealists, who regarded the everyday world as alienation brought on by routine yet still filled with possibility, the difference in the same— imagined it as the place of transformation and "religious experience," what he labeled "profane illumination."[54]

The surrealist intervention was based on pursuing the everyday itself as the path for turning it inside out, which matched Benjamin's earlier desire to break through the commodity form in order to restore its forgotten history—and, thereby, to transform the residues from the "space of time" into the "dream of time." In this way, he hoped to see through what he called a "Copernican Revolution of remembrance" (*Passages*, pp. 405–406; *K*, pp. 1, 1).

> The Copernican Revolution in this vision of history consists in this. One will consider another time—[*das Gewesene*] (not simply the past opposed to the now) as a fixed point and one thinks that the present tries to pull itself up to the knowledge of this fixed element. Henceforth, this relationship should reverse itself and the other time becomes a dialectical reversal and an irruption of the awakened conscience. Politics takes precedence over History. (*Passages*, p. 405)

This revolution comes from within modernity itself, not from the repetition of tradition (Heidegger) or an unrealized social or cultural form. Benjamin's method for realizing this program lay in his conception of "construction" (with anecdote, quotation, etc.), appealing to the form of the montage rather than the narrative— the prisoner of historicism—which now has appeared as a dying form no longer capable of communicating historical experience.

In his earliest (1927) foray into constructing the experience of everyday life, "One Way Street," Benjamin described his program:

> The construction of life is at present in the power far more than of facts than of convictions, and of such facts as have scarcely ever become the basis of convictions. Under these circumstances, true literary activity cannot aspire to take place within a literary

framework. Significant literary effectiveness can come into being only in a strict alternation between action and writings; it must nurture the inconspicuous forms that fits influence in active communities better than does the pretentious, universal gesture of the book, in leaflets, brochures, and placards.[55]

Elsewhere, he observed how the objects of daily use were repelling him and the immense labor "there was to perform" in "overcoming the sum of secret resistances." This stance was more fully articulated in Benjamin's essay on surrealism which, it is important to recall, is subtitled "The Last Snapshot of the European Intelligentsia."

> Any serious exploration of occult, phantasmagoric gifts and phenomena presupposes a dialectical intertwinement to which a romantic turn of mind is impervious. For histrionic or fanatical stress on the mysterious side of the mysterious takes us no further; we penetrate the mystery only to the degree that we recognize it in the everyday world, by virtue of a dialectical optic that perceives the everyday as impenetrable, the impenetrable as everyday.[56]

If the surrealist project aimed at transforming daily objects in order to release their aesthetic consciousness, Benjamin, struggling to fill the present with the now, tried to modify this program for historical materialism by removing it to liberate historical energy, much as he tried to do in his excavations of nineteenth-century Paris. This redefinition of art, standing in for culture, worked politically to transform the everyday into a historical experience. It was in this sense that the Copernican revolution of remembrance was realized and how in the dialectical relationship between the then and the now "politics takes precedence over history." Activating the present depended on an act of mourning, remembering what had been forgotten in the past, which lay in a dormant state waiting to be summoned to the present as form of political praxis. What Benjamin managed to accomplish, despite the abortiveness of his own program, was to bring politics and everyday life—in which both surrealism and contemporary cultural studies, each in their own way, have shown an interest, even though the intensity has differed— into an active relationship by theorizing Marxism again in order to discern its possibilities.[57] This task was, I believe, actualized by Henri Lefebvre, who disavowed the surrealist dimensions (even though he was clearly affected by them) and sought to replace the strategy of turning the everyday inside out with the recognition of unevenness and the alienation it reinforced as the basis of a research program. Although he acknowledged the importance of Heidegger's text while holding back on its significance of treating everydayness existentially for subsequent, systematic analysis, Lefebvre was also convinced that the "paroxysmal moment (Heidegger's moment of vision) dispossesses mundane everyday existence, annulling it, destroying it. It is the very thing which denies life; it is the nothingness of anguish, of vertigo, of fascination."[58] For Lefebvre, everyday life had become the "verso of modernity, the spirit of our time," quoting Hermann Broch, through which the difficult labor of exorcising the "ghost of revolution" would begin.[59]

With Lefebvre, as well as Tosaka Jun, everydayness manifested a mode of temporalizing that was different from the modern mode combining the presentness of the Heideggerian now and repetition. At one level, everydayness thus served as the intersection of all repetitions, both received and recent, past and modern, the site of "recurrences," by which he meant "gestures of labor and leisure, mechanical movements both human and properly mechanic, hours, days, weeks, months, years, linear and cyclical repetitions." It was also "material culture," clothing (especially for Tosaka), life, furniture, houses, neighborhoods, environment—the solidity of filled space, Heidegger's "there" (Da), the world of the present. If this is what Lefebvre (and Pessoa) referred to as the "veiled," hidden, shadow existence, the modern, by contrast, revealed this everydayness in its immediacy. "The quotidian," he wrote, "is what is humble and solid, what is taken for granted," an unvarying succession of todays and tomorrows and predictable sequences, the "undated" and "insignificant."[60] As "practically untellable," it meets the modern, which now appears as the endlessly novel, worldly, transitory, and spectacular. In this momentous encounter, the new—strategically "misrepresented as modernity," which, according to Peter Osborne, is an ideological misrecognition for the reproduction of capital accumulation—functions as "repetitive gestures" masking the regular cycles of everyday life as the "monotony of everydayness constrains the new." In this explosive encounter of repetitions, "everything changes."[61]

3. "DIALECTICAL OPTICS"

History in Everydayness

We shall unify [our existence] as a doubled layered life in the whole-
ness [zentai] of everyday life.
— Watsuji Tetsurō, *Zoku Nihonseishinshi kenkyū*

The everyday escapes. This is its definition. . . . The everyday is always
unrealized in its very actualization which no event, however important
or insignificant, can ever produce.
— Maurice Blanchot

Fantasizing Everyday Life

In many ways, the interwar experience of Japan's modernization
appeared as a doubling and reworking through the logic of historical repetition whose first run was through the United States and
western Europe. The Japanese experience showed, especially for
subsequent examples labeled as "alternative modernities," that
modernity was always a doubling that imprinted the difference
between the demands of capitalism and the force of received forms
of history and culture — the culture of reference now challenged by
the establishment of a new mode of production — in the space of
everyday life. This was not necessarily the double consciousness
envisaged by W. E. B. DuBois but surely the establishment of a kind
of life satisfying the requirements of the new political economy and
the coexistence or coevalness of received forms, what Lefebvre saw
as the "inherence of productive activity in [peasant] life in its
entirety."[1] If modernity means destroying this culture of reference
to reterritorialize society, the result is to remake society to look like
every other place but not quite the same because of the particular
inflections produced by the encounter between the new and the ves-
tiges of another time that never went away. When Partha Chaterjee

complained that the formerly colonized are destined to be nothing more than perpetual "consumers of modernity," there can only be one response. It is still possible, however, to show that the doubling produces genuine differences that do not derive their force from an uncontaminated sanctuary of pure culture that has remained immune to modernity. The Japanese literary critic Kobayashi Hideo commented in the 1930s that the modernizing process resembled Marx's reworking of the Hegelian observation that history the first time was tragedy, and the second time it was comedy. Such a view hinged on accepting the proposition that Japan was just a pale imitation of Europe's modern history.

During the interwar period, Japanese Marxists insisted that because Japan was a "latecomer" to modernization, it had sacrificed the transformation of domains like the social, political, and cultural for economic and technological development. As a result, Japanese society lagged behind the more fully developed nations, as it still was plagued by feudal legacies and thus destabilizing social contradictions that sent the country into absolutism, militarism, and fascism. After World War II, modernizers like the social theorist Maruyama Masao, who followed the Marxists' scenario, even though he was not one, constantly argued that Japan's modernity was incomplete, thereby implying a normative model against which its sameness or difference might be measured. The literary and cultural critic Takeuchi Yoshimi condemned Japan for aping the West and pointed to the Chinese communists as an example that Japan should follow because they neither copied the modern West nor relied on reified traditional forms. If Maruyama misrecognized difference for incompleteness (he also proposed that war and defeat offered Japan a second chance at modernity), Takeuchi misperceived completion as copy. The very incompleteness that thinkers discerned in Japan's modern history was, in fact, a sign of modernity itself. This, as Benjamin observed and the Japanese confirmed, was "precisely the modern which conjures up prehistory."[2]

It is important to distinguish between a literature that rarely problematized the incomplete character of modernity in Europe, which merely assumed that it was being lived, and one, dramatized by the Japanese, that made both the time lag and its unfinished status a principal condition of all discussions of modernity, accepted by both Japanese and non-Japanese alike. The paradox of this view is that even between the wars, Japan probably lagged behind only the United States, which has never questioned its status as a completed modernity. I can only hint at what this conceit has done to scholarship and its consequences for Japanese political thought.

Because everydayness was produced by the transformations demanded by capitalism, it was made to look uniform everywhere it took root. This sense of homogeneity matched the existential conception of everydayness that saw it primordially as the "first" and "foremost" mode in which Being discloses itself to itself. Presumably, Being's history was the same everywhere. Heidegger, it should be remembered, imagined everyday life as the least differentiated and determinate expression of Being's existence, which accounts for his lack of sociological specificity. "This undifferentiated character of Dasein's everydayness," he noted, "is not nothing, but a phenomenal characteristic of this entity. Out of this kind of Being — and back into it again — is all existing, such as it is" (BT, p. 69).

Among the many Japanese philosophers who had studied with Heidegger, such as Kuki Shūzō, Tanabe Hajime, and Miki Kiyoshi, this lack of determinate character was the informing principle of everyday life and the starting point for phenomenological reflection, even if it required thematization and sociological and historical differentiation in the final analysis. If, as Peter Osborne suggested, everyday life is an "unavoidable category" (Lefebvre's "the quotidian is unavoidable . . .") because it was not originally thematized — constituting its mode of presentation before reflection — this "primordial" account of Being's everyday life is also the "starting point" for all subsequent reflection. It is the later reflection — the "kind of Being" that flows back into all existence — reaching an end point that gives it significance and thereby opens the way for "informing and transforming everydayness." Despite Heidegger's guarded effort to keep this conception of everydayness free from sociological content, both his views concerning the dictatorship of the masses and his distrust of democracy slipped through. The narrative from inauthentic back to authentic existence itself opened the way to rethink, refigure, and recontextualize everydayness in historically specific forms "out of which and back into which" all existing goes, at particular times in particular places.[3] This move was already evident in Benjamin's program and was developed more fully in Lefebvre.

The Japanese experience with modernity and everydayness before the war showed that the two were linked but still separate and that everyday life was inescapably caught in the unevenness of old cycles of routine and ritual and new cycles of work and consumption. Although Japan embarked on a program of capitalist modernization in the 1870s, it was not until World War I and the decades until World War II that the industrial transformation was accelerated. At this time, Japan, in part because of its involvement in the war as a supplier to the Allies, shifted from light- to heavy-capital industries and from the status of a debtor to that of a creditor nation. Its ratio of agricultural to industrial labor began to change quantitatively, and the great metropolitan sites like Tokyo/Yokohama and Osaka/Kobe began to parallel cities in the capitalist West. Recording the experience of everyday life itself and how the space and temporality of the new coexisted and mingled with a prehistory signaled the very history that produced it. More often than not, this "history" was often "forgotten" or absent in the texts that announced the establishment of novelty and fashion.

Modernization transformed historical cities like Tokyo into massive centers of manufacturing, exchange, communication, and cultural production. In the early twentieth century, the cities drew large numbers of immigrants from the surrounding countryside, providing them with work and shelter in crowded centers where they were strangers to one another and to themselves. Both the native ethnologist Yanagita Kunio and the detective story writer Edogawa Rampo observed that Tokyo in the 1920s was a city filled with foreigners and that the familiar symmetries associated with an older style of life were disappearing, forming immense pockets of unevenness with the newly emerging structures and patterns of capitalist life.

Capitalist modernization in Japan, as elsewhere, projected the image of an uneven terrain of development between the cities and the countryside, the home country and the colonies. Its law of motion demanded that some sectors develop at the expense of others, despite its ideological promise of eventual even development everywhere. Yanagita devoted a book to examining the consequences of this spectacle. *Toshi to nōson* (The city and the village, 1929) documents in great detail the enormous disparities the state had produced between city and countryside. But others noticed, as he did in his historically symbolic text *Meiji Taishōshi, sesōhen* (1931) (History of custom in the Meiji and Taishō periods), that this unevenness was particularly evident in the large cities, where new forces of production and social relationships were often made to coexist uneasily and unhappily with older forms of production and their own preferences for social identity.

Yanagita was describing Tokyo after World War I as a place of broken kin relationships, but he could have been writing about other cities elsewhere.

The loneliness of life in the early days of the city depended on making people travelers, yearning for families long absent. But the effect of putting too much emphasis on one's home village was that the cities were filled with residents who were not attached to anywhere at any time.[4]

The German social theorist Ernst Bloch conceptualized the qualitative differences he observed in the countryside in the Weimar period as "nonsynchronisms," in which people lived different kinds of existence in different temporalities at the same time, which offered fascism its recruiting ground. In Japan especially, the recognition of the cultural heterogeneity lived and experienced was a constant reminder of the unevenness in economic development and thus the necessity of forging, as Yanagita and others tried to do, a homogeneous national identity devoid of class, gender, and sexuality and capable of unifying the differences and fragments produced by modernity.

This cultural unevenness was dramatized by the expanding metropolitan sites and its discourse by contemporaries on everydayness, called first *bunka seikatsu* (cultural life) or everyday culture.

New media like popular and illustrated magazines, mass newspapers and tabloids, the movies, and radio constituted a discourse that actually formed the figure of everyday life. Advertisements and articles promoted the vision of modern life through the lure of commodities such as the radio, phonograph, telephone, "cultural houses" for salarymen and their families, and cars, announcing the ceaseless changes in material life introduced by new consumer products and the circulation of a conception of life based on the new and on fashion. The discourse constantly pointed to both the succession of events, as the making of eventfulness became the principal commodity of newspapers and popular magazines aimed at new identity groups, and the concomitant fragmentation and destabilization of older cultural forms. Yet the swift succession of events, like the constant circulation of commodities in which the new and presumably different replaced the old, which was quickly forgotten, showed only that everydayness was a space exceeding the capability of any event to produce or represent it. This reflective discourse provoked by the appearance and practice of new forms of everyday life was more important than the actual ubiquity of the new everydayness, because it signified the formation of an experiential realm beginning to be lived that would expand in the future. Just as important, it pointed to a historical situation that would figure a fantasy life and what Benjamin called a "phantasmagoria" that demanded fulfillment but that, like the commodity form and the constant "flair for fashion," is never completed, realized, finished.

For Japanese, modernity was speed, shock, succession, and the spectacle of sensation. These qualities were often symbolized in subjectivities like the "modern girl," "Marx boy," "Engels girl," and the cafe waitress. During the 1920s, the new images were often characterized as the "feminization of culture," according to the Marxian critic Hirabayashi Hatsunosuke. "We hear through the phone receiver women's voices in conversations that ask 'What number?' Women are riding on trams as conductors who punch your tickets, and self-confident women typists work in offices and banks. Even in small businesses you can't miss detecting the presence of the new personnel." The same was true of schools and hospitals. Women's voices were now heard everywhere, and women were seen everywhere, in art museums, department stores, and publishing houses and making up a large proportion of workers in textile plants and other industries.[5] In an earlier essay written in 1926, Hirabayashi worried about the "slave status" that capitalism had forced on women. This identification of women in everyday life and work was merely a reminder, however, of the overdetermination of the figure of the "modern girl" (*modan gāru*) itself and what this meant for Japanese society. The new roles assumed by women signaled, as nothing else, the changes beginning to take place in the world of modern experience. (It is interesting to recall that Kracauer estimated in his *Die Angestellten* that women constituted more than a third of Berlin's working population.) Overdetermination, which dominated the discourse on everydayness, was the sign of its historicity.

The idea of "cultural living" was promoted first by the state which, immediately after World War I, launched the daily life reform movement (*seikatsu kaizen undō*) or the simple life movement (*shimpuru raifu undō*). It was inspired by the French bestseller *La vie simple* (1917), which was translated from an American work. The purpose of the movement, which ultimately metamorphosed into mass-commodity culture called "modern life," or simply "*seikatsu*," was to control the newly emerging everyday life being imagined and figured in the new popular media and beginning to be lived in the cities. This meant implementing a program that would simultaneously emphasize rationality and efficiency and economies and yet caution people from becoming too deeply involved in the culture of commodities.[6] In fact, the state momentarily tried to prevent consumers from being interpellated by the commodity (recalling Benjamin's fantasy that if the commodity had a soul, "it would be the most empathetic ever encountered"). While one of the proponents of cultural living, Morimoto Atsuyoshi, was convinced that daily life had to be rationalized, the decision to distinguish mere "existence" (*seizon*) from "living" (*seikatsu*) as the mark of progressive civilization undermined the desire to "manage national life" by opening the doors to the mass consumption of new household commodities that easily exceeded the needs of an efficient household. Cultural living was communicated by advertisements for new products like irons; phonographs; radios; kitchen labor-saving devices; Western-style skirts, dresses, and trousers (all cheaply made and seen as more efficient wear); new foods that promised better nourishment and health at lower prices; and new apartments and "culture houses" that could accommodate the salaryman and his family (white-collar workers in the city), all offering "convenience," "utility," and "economy."[7]

All these new commodities pointed to the acquisition of new identities that often traversed class, gender, and sexuality, even though "cultural living" was at first limited to the urban middle class. What started out as a culture of efficiency and economy for the white-collar class became a culture of the masses who worked in urban-based industries, consumed its products, and played on its streets. In fact, the discourse on everydayness was really centered on the streets (recalling, once more, Benjamin's observations concerning the centrality of the streets in nineteenth-century Paris.) The social researcher Gonda Yasunosuke, who spent a good deal of time in the streets, saw "everyday life" as an extension of the streets, as one form of "*strasse*," as he called it. The street for him represented an expanded stage filled with a moving montage of cars, walkers, shops, vendors, movie houses, dance halls, and bars. When the heroes of "modern life," the modern girl and boy, were forced to return to their homes, he remarked, "it was like cutting off the whiskers of a cat."[8] The urban ethnographer Kon Wajirō, about whom more will be said shortly, observed in numerous studies carried out in the 1920s and early 1930s the multiple identities produced on the streets and played out on every corner and place where people could congregate and enact the behavior of a different subjectivity. In this regard, the streets were empowering. Life on the streets constantly externalized the power of desire and the way people acted out their innermost fantasies, as if they were crowded on a theater stage. (This metaphor was in fact used by Kon.) Terms like *gaito* (street), *minshū* (people), and *taishū* (masses) entered the lexicon of common buzzwords that were used everywhere in speech and writing and came to be associated with people moving on the streets, consuming new products and forms of entertainment.

In Japan, as elsewhere, as the memory of the war and its deprivations receded, the heroism of production was replaced by the heroism of consumption, which resulted not so much in a clash between newer and established values as in a struggle of desire against value itself. The pleasures offered by the new commodity culture—the "philosophy of fun" celebrated by Gonda—however exaggerated and overdetermined in social discourse and limited to the middle class—still attested to the social practices and lived experience in the phenomenological present that alone gave direction to history, which was the everyday. This everydayness, always ready to explode into history and the rapid succession of events— the ever-new in the ever-same—was dramatized in the appeal to American material culture and its cinematic representations and in yet another overdetermined figure proclaimed and denounced as "Americanism." Its hero was the "modern girl" (moga), a combination of Clara Bow flapper and women who had entered the new industrial workforce and urban labor market and realized for the first time a measure of autonomy and financial independence.

In 1942, at the time of the Kyoto Conference on Overcoming the Modern, one of the organizers, Kawakami Tetsutarō, called attention to this figure as a "laughable species devoted to Americanism" but nonetheless acknowledged the threat it already posed to received patterns of social relationships.[9] The fear that spread through the interwar period and was inscribed in the production of cultural theory was the recognition that everyday life was reproducing patterns of existence and experience that were antiquating the most recent past and repudiating precisely those mechanisms of received social relationships that had once generated a fixed culture of repeated identities, a concrete historical experience that had become routinized into "second nature" and involuntary memory. In Hirabayashi's view, women, who had once been confined to the household—"interiorized," as he put it—were now "exteriorized" to participate fully in modern society's multiple processes. The figure of the modern girl challenged the function of reproduction itself, traditionally identified with women, and gave further meaning to the "feminization of culture," which came to mean the culture of modernity rather than culture as reproduction (biological and socio-political), lived rather than recalled, performative rather than constative.

As early as 1918, the influential opinion journal *Chūō kōron* (Central review) ran a special issue on modernity that sought the "symbolic currents of the new age" and found them in new images like the "automobile," "moving pictures," and the "cafe." A decade later, the playwright Kikuchi Kan proclaimed that "true modernity, made in Japan, was just beginning," and the proof lay in the appearance of "new women and men" and the "birth of a new human being."[10] In this historical moment, the critic Uchida Roan reported—in the same issue on modernity—that "after the war, the cream of milk skimmed off in department stores and motion pictures was American capitalism," which later he described as an "essential something that had caught the public spirit."

In its capacity to de-territorialize, capitalism simply "undermined every fixed identity" and produced innumerable subject positions and ambiguous inflections, all challenging the fixity of received and traditional roles. Novelists like Tanizaki Junichirō, Kawabata Yasunari, and especially the detective story writer Edogawa Rampo explored new sexual identities and their consequences for settled social relationships. In discourse, "all seemed captivated by the modern girl and were drawn to her hairstyle, clothing, attitude, facial and bodily movements, and her way of walking." The figure of the *moga* (who with the *mobo*—modern boy—paralleled a transformation of the late Tokugawa heroic couple of the pleasure quarters—the *tsūjin* and *tayu*) appeared in a short skirt worn ten centimeters above the knees, Clara Bow haircut, lipstick, and rouge, a woman who "struts through throngs" signifying both sexual and financial independence. Tanizaki Junichirō's portrayal of the modern girl in *Chijin no ai* (1931) is a cafe waitress who "resembled the motion picture actress Mary Pickford: there was something definitely Western about her appearance."[11] An exaggerated image, to be sure, but one that magnified the limits or extremities of new behavior and the excitement and danger it elicited. Kikuchi Kan pointed to these "new women" as representing a new sexual awakening and declared that their appearance marked the beginning of a new modernity in 1927.

"Young women," he wrote, "have become unusually empowered at this time, and they . . . are able to 'cross swords' with men in matters of love." Kikuchi, and others, was attesting to the prominence of these liberated and independent women in such areas as work and sexuality that had once been monopolized by a patriarchal system, one that cultural theory desperately tried to preserve. Uchida Roan recognized the genuinely erotic behavior of the modern girl in her manner of "pouting" and "scowling" that "elicited widespread emulation." He also observed that it "would be difficult to understand the modern girl and modern boy without seeing American movies."[12]

For many, the film was the principal vehicle that conveyed the "textbook lessons" for modern Japan's everyday life. One writer was convinced that motion pictures had a great cultural influence on Japanese society because it "imposed a Westernization of depth rather than one of surfaces." Now, according to another commentator, the people (*minshū*) might spend a lot of time laughing in movie houses, but he was sure that "they understood well this thing called the West." "My favorite among the symbols of modernity," wrote the poet Satō Haruo, "is the motion pictures. When I reflect on them, I feel duty bound to live in the present."[13] Hirabayashi ranked the cinema, along with sports and Marxism, as the great "phenomena of the present." And Kikuchi Kan confessed that "even if one watches four or five hours a day, one does so cheerfully." He would gladly watch anything with a Western content rather than sit through a Japanese film. More than either Japanese or European imports, American films centered a culture of commodity consumption and the ever-present demands of desire fed by the ever-new. The film critic Tsumura Hideo observed that the sweeping success of American films throughout Asia derived from the power of capital and its presentation of a world of commodities—"cultural living"—and the obvious fact that American films were preponderantly Westerns and "slapstick comedies" with little easily understood dialogue. Film was not just a sign of capitalism because it was a leading industry exporting a product and driving out all competition (especially the French). According to Tsumura, it also displayed a commodity culture produced by American capitalism and its main subjects, modern women and men and their customs and experience of everyday life. (When I first went to Japan, I rented a room in a house owned by a man who, even as late as the early 1960s, everyday tried to make himself look like Charlie Chaplin before he left the house!)

Although many observers of the scene recommended films as the best way to understand the everyday life, others saw that it could be understood concretely and immediately in newspapers and mass-circulation magazines and in new forms of popular music imported from the United States. The first issue (October 1930) of *Modern Japan* (Modan Nippon) celebrated a litany of modern customs, material things, and images that its readers would soon be seeing, such as "flush toilets," "pavement," "Western clothes," "chairs," "apartments," and "business suits." Moreover, life would be more "sporty" and "speedy"; "there would be more respect for women and a downgrading of men"; and people would be hearing more "jazz," and seeing more "women's legs" and "breasts." A later issue of *Modern Japan* and the Kōdansha popular magazine *King* praised the "Yankee spirit" and welcomed it and "American daily life" to Japan. Other publications reported on the culture of glimmering neon lights and the steady march of people from dance halls to jazz joints and crowds of people drinking hard in cafes, spilling into the streets, and scurrying off in one-yen taxi cabs on "broadened thoroughfares"—Gonda's *"strasse"* constructed after the earthquake of 1923. Social discourse in magazines like *Shufu no tomo* described the new "culture houses" of salarymen, the appearance of nuclear families living in the cities, their household economies and outdoor recreation such as excursions to parks and miniature golf links and leisure time spent with the family milling through department stores stocked with affordable commodities like cameras, radios, irons, and phonographs.

Aono Suekichi is, like Kracauer in Germany, our best guide to the lifestyles of the new middle class, their aspirations, fears, and punctured expectations after 1929, what he called their "panic." In the late 1930s, the women's magazine *Fujin kōron* printed transcripts of discussions in which Japan's most prominent male and female intellectuals and writers assessed the status of the new "living culture" (*seikatsu bunka*), as it was increasingly called. One discussion concentrated on the utility of the bed and the bedroom, in contrast to the tatami room and futon. Opinion heavily favored the bed. The 1920s also saw the explosion of a kid's culture consisting of new products targeted to children, such as phonographs, records, toys, miniature trains, telescopes, and new candies produced by Meiji and Morinaga. Children even had their own magazine, which imitated the more popular women's journals like *Shufu no tomo* and *Josei*. But because the social discourse on everyday life was concerned with surface descriptions—literally advertising, tracking, and figuring the establishment and circulation of a new material reality—it also began to reveal doubts about the consequences of the conquest of commodity culture and complain about the effects of unevenness, "superficiality" (Ōya Sōichi), and visible social contradictions at about the same time the Japanese army was occupying Manchuria. In fact, the expansion of the Japanese empire should be counted as both signifying the recognition of this unevenness and the principal social contradiction of Japan's capitalist modernization. One of the responses to this growing concern with the social disequilibrium caused by the commodity culture (and imperialism) was to mitigate its effects by appealing to the priority of a culture often resembling Heidegger's primordial everydayness, removed from the differentiations of modern society, a culture of depth that has left its traces in the present.

Customizing the Space of Everydayness

The discourse on everyday life was constructed in the new media for mass consumption, overdetermining objects, figures, and images along the way. Social thinkers drew on this vast inventory to imagine a new social reality that, they believed, would eventually permeate all sectors of Japanese life. While it was true that everyday life was identified closely with the industrializing cities, most observers believed that it would become a principal and permanent figure of social life in the future. This belief explains why so much activity in the interwar period was invested in seeing every-day life as the basis of a new social space and why so many thinkers looked for lasting alternatives to its social contradictions and the shadow of unevenness it cast with its ceaseless construction of con-ceptions of fixed community and culture. In the 1920s and 1930s, the first reflex was to determine the meaning of this experience of lived existence. The crisis of modern life in Japan and elsewhere was thus one of meaning, which called into question the rela-tionship between forms of communicating experience, namely, historical narrative and discourse and lived reality.

In this secondary discourse, which I have named *dialectical optics*, from Benjamin's interpretation of how surrealists penetrated the mystery of everyday life, the present was seen as a foreground, often as the place where traditions were shattered, provoking a cri-sis in the communication of experience itself, in memory, and in the very possibility of historical recall. Both novelistic fiction and social discourse began to shed developmental dispositions that had been at the basis of their production but were now undermining them, bringing with them and embracing new forms of commu-nication and temporal experience. Hence, the *shishōsetsu* — the "I" novel — and the various discursive efforts to displace history show that historical narrative — the developmental form — had lost its liv-ing relationship to the present — the place of *seikatsu* — as the form of "memorative communication."

Instead, writers and thinkers like Kon Wajirō, Aono Suekichi, Gonda Yasunosuke, Tosaka Jun, and Hirabayashi Hatsunosuke dis-tanced themselves from a memorative past, as such, and the demand for narrating its historical conditions of existence in fixed periods for an engagement of the performative present. Others like Kuki Shūzō, Watsuji Tetsurō, Tanizaki Junichirō, and all those Edo viewers of the 1920s looked to a moment in the past that would serve as the primordial or original condition of existence of the Japanese folk. Between these two extremes was Kobayashi Hideo, who rejected history altogether but sought to identify the commonness of everyday life that historical narrative missed as the experience binding past to present. This optical refraction showed the central-

ity of everyday life in explaining the present and as the key to grasping Japan's modern historical experience in the future. Kon Wajirō
overstated an observation that the overwhelming engagement of
and enthusiasm for everydayness in the 1920s and 1930s in Japan
contrasted dramatically with the Europeans, who had not yet explicitly thematized this dimension of modern life. But when Tosaka Jun
proposed that everyday life supplied the informing principle for
both the experience of space and time, Gonda announced that
people's pleasures derived from the experience of everyday life on
the streets and the accessibility of new forms of entertainment, and
Kon insisted that the site of everydayness and its transactions in
home and on the streets was the source of subjectivity. Here, we
have not the simple expressions of enthusiasm for "modern life" but
instances of what it had come to mean to Japanese living in a present that was incomplete but constantly opening up to unimagined
possibilities. No writer showed better the dilemmas and frustrations
experienced by a whole class of people in this new modern setting
than Aono Suekichi, who recorded the growing estrangement of
Japan's petite bourgeoisie as their aspirations overtook their capacity to fulfill them. Modern custom was seen as rationality and
rational expectations, and people were now, for the first time, in a
position to make choices for themselves. As Tosaka had charged,
philosophy had begun to distance itself from this performative present by narrativizing the historical conditions of existence in ways
that fixed the real life of Japanese in historical periods, risking mis-
reading of the past and confusing an abstract reality (*genjitsu*) for
concrete actuality. Others, however, saw modern life as rational,
efficient, and even scientific, requiring a flow of information and
knowledge.

Where Japanese like Tosaka and Hirabayashi differed from
people like Benjamin and Heidegger, but not Kracauer, was in
their confidence in journalism, newspapers, and magazines, which
contrasted with academic discourses disregarding everyday life and
the concrete as serious categories for a conception of abstract "reality" or false concreteness. This does not mean that Tosaka and Kracauer were not critical of journalistic practices and their reliance

on immediate observation and dismissal of the role played by mediation in the production of meaning. Rather, they saw everydayness
increasingly as what was left over from the public realm, the
residue left by the world of state and society that had no everyday
and was thus its opposite, its negative, which it tried to discount
by insisting on the "official" separation of public and private. Transforming everyday life was considered to be the fundamental condition for remodeling society itself, for altering received political
and social relationships in the name of science and rationality and
its capability to realize the possibilities offered by the experience
of the present.

The most recognizable sign of engaging a performative present was the formation of a discipline by the architect Kon Wajirō
in the 1920s, named *kōgengaku*, which he translated as "moder-
nologio." This discipline immediately disclosed a powerful desire
to catch hold of and describe the experience of the streets and the
best method of realizing it. Although thinkers like Tosaka denounced *kōgengaku* for its phenomenological formalism, it nonetheless tried to make sense—by concentrating on the role of modern custom in negotiating this new life—of everyday life in the
cities, especially after the earthquake of 1923, that was being lived
but also was always escaping. Here Tosaka paradoxically resembled Kon inasmuch as both wanted to concentrate on the status
of custom as the totalizing form through which to understand the
character and meaning of modern life.

For Kon, this meant describing modern custom and its relationship to new subjectivities, and for Tosaka, it was seeing custom as a stand-in for the commodity form, going beyond mere
description to penetrate what lay behind custom and convention
in order to understand the possibilities for changing everyday life.
Both, as well as others, saw the key to everyday life as its relationship to custom and convention, routinized practices. "Our research
object," Kon announced, "avoids the abnormal. In general, it's
about the everyday life of society and its people."[14] In addition,
kōgengaku had become a "study of consumption in life." Kon saw
the buying of "commodities" as an integral part of understanding
daily life, one of its main constituents and not just a whim of curios-

ity. Research showed that there was a regular imitation in patterns of consumption, a transaction marked by a "wave of custom in which the upper class is imitated," the practice of mimicry observed earlier by the French sociologist Gabriel Tarde (with whose work Kon was acquainted) among the lower classes who usually aped the customs of the upper class. Tarde saw this relationship mediated by the force of imitation and mimicry as a guarantee of social solidarity, whereas Kon presented it as a demand for differing customs and commodities made available on a mass scale, indeed as a sign of progressive rationalization in the sphere of consumption. What interested him was the constant flow of goods and people and their endless circulation. It was at this juncture that Kon, fearing complete commodification, turned to the solution offered earlier by Boris Arbatov, which was already circulating in the texts of Japan's constructivists.

In this scene, Arbatov had offered the idea of subjectivity and, what seemed to him, the inexhaustible number of subject positions that people occupy in their everyday encounters. Therefore the discipline of "modernology" attempted to deal with commodities as "use objects," privileging their functionality and utility. Even though they appear to be the same, each must be seen from a different angle of vision. Places that demand investigation should begin with the household, since the family is the principal component of social structure. Research on how objects are specifically used in these environments would, Kon believed, bring out the "social meaning contained within these commodities," even though it was not apparent on the surface (Fuzoku, pp. 14–15). Actors or buyers produced different meanings with the commodities they purchased, inasmuch as they entered into these transactions with specific uses in mind. Here Kon advanced a conception of subjectivity based on the presumption that people who buy were in the best position to know what they wanted and why. That is, they would act on a knowledge that told them which object they should buy and why it would be useful. Consumption was linked to conscious decisions identifying utility and its value, and the buyer who possessed this knowledge was empowered to act as a consumer.

Kon's investigations were based on intensive observations of people in different locations, such as public spaces, streets, and parks. Once there, he focused on conduct and clothing and indeed all the material details of everyday life. He was not just gathering information but also accumulating a knowledge of contemporary custom that might be transmitted as a "beneficial" legacy to the future. In this connection, Kon brought up again the desire of contemporary native ethnologists, who, driven by the impulse to conserve, carried out research on the surviving traces and residual practices of folk life, to preserve and transmit timeless custom as an act of memoration. By contrast, the past for Kon was eclipsed by the present, the now, and seemed to recede in his own considerations, as evidenced by his views on the rebuilding of Tokyo after the earthquake. Instead, he looked to constructing a storehouse of memory for the future based on the experience of the present rather than to communicating the memory of a past that reminded the present of what they had lost.

What was so extraordinary about Kon's program was his desire to transform the present social formation into a temporality he called *gendai*, the contemporary, similar to Tosaka's conception of the "now" (*ima*), a moment that seemed to have no connection to the past and stretched out to an indeterminate future. This move was prompted by the Tokyo earthquake of 1923, a cataclysmic event that literally tore large parts of the city from its Edo past, and its aftermath, which saw both the reconstruction of the city and the acceleration of mass society with its greater importation of American material culture. The necessity of rebuilding the city and the rapid circulation of American material culture introducing the ever-new into Japanese life after 1924 persuaded Kon to propose that new economic and political conditions now dictated that burned-out sites should not be reconstructed in their original form. Rather, the past lay in the ashes of the burned fields he and his associate (Yoshida Kenkichi) had walked through when they first envisioned the new program of "modernology." Hence, he imagined the contemporary as a "moving present" (*ugoki tsutsu aru*) "developing before one's eyes." "If you take a step outside the door, you'll see the spectacle that will be the object [of investigation]" (Fuzoku, p. 1).[15] But grasping and describing it, he acknowledged, would be difficult.

The form in which Kon wished to communicate this experience eschewed narrative (much as Yanagita Kunio did in his studies of folk life) for detailed reports profusely illustrated with drawings and sketches he made on location. These illustrations usually were drawings of, say, hats worn by pedestrians, hairstyles, clothing, and the like, making up both an inexhaustible inventory of contemporary custom and an archive of multiple practices denoting a knowledge of the "moving present." When he sought to explain his discipline's difference from other forms of anthropological and ethnographic inquiry, he distinguished modernology from archaeology by noting that the latter was bound to history while the former was not, as it aimed to unearth the present rather than the past. It was best exemplified in the approach characterizing his *Tokyotogai fūzoku zatsushū* (1925) which often resembled a documentary montage rather than a historical narrative. In this report, Kon described "customs" as they appeared on the streets of Ginza at certain times of the day, demonstrating what was called *Ginzabura*, which included observations that measured the ratio of people looking at show windows, noting changes according to the time of day, ages, gender, occupations of people strolling through the area, styles of dress, and hairstyle.[16] He readily acknowledged that these phenomenal observations alone did not explain the discipline of modernology, which would have consigned its function to mere observational description.[17]

The details documented from Ginza life supplied an image of contemporary lived existence, a historical image of the present, that served as a metonymical stand-in for the unenvisioned whole of everyday life. Kon confessed to a personal interest in the "actual investigation of everyday life" that evolved from his growing dissatisfaction with studying rural life and the designs of folk houses. The earthquake jolted him into deciding to change the site of his investigation to the immediate present ("an actual investigation of everyday life") instead of examining the styles of rural farmhouses derived from the past and the people who inhabited this moment whose lives "were contained in it." In other words, he moved the site of investigation from artifacts of the past and place to the time of the present and space of the city. Assisted by a friend, an artist who eventually "fled that capital of death," Kon wandered around the scene of destruction and walked "on the ground of burned fields everyday." "I rejoiced over the fact that I was recording various things actually seen by the eye," he reported, as if any other form of mediated research could never exceed representation (Fuzoku, p. 6). His own reflexive awareness of being there and observing the scene, his desire to situate himself in the site of investigation, was an appeal to the authority of the eyewitness who authenticates his own claim to occupy the position of the subject who knows. By the same token, Kon acknowledged that the subjectivity of the observer was not always distinguishable from that of the observed.

Compared with Simmel, Kon recognized the distance between an empirical, objective world and the interior subjective self but sought to overcome its aporetic relationship by implementing a research program that put him in the immediacy of the scene, whether it was the glittering world of Ginza shops stocked with alluring commodities interpellating people or the shantytown of Fukugawa, whose "beneficial knowledge" of a lived experience would be transmitted to later generations. The purpose of *kogengaku* was to make the "effort to record and analyze contemporary custom before it became history," before it disappeared into a discarded and completed past. Yet Kon was convinced that the act of understanding contemporary custom wrote another kind of history whose relevance could be used by future generations. This meant capturing custom as it was being lived and experienced before it hardened into habitual convention. While recognizing that his discipline relied on the application of sociological techniques rooted in an awareness of the now of everyday life, he was satisfied that it was sufficiently different from the social scientific practices of the West, since it concentrated on the present, the immediacy of custom and subjectivity. "Temporally," he wrote, "our modernology is opposed to archaeology; spatially it is opposed to native ethnology. It aims to study the everyday life of the modern man of culture" (Fuzoku, p. 5). Closely recalling the documentary montage captured in Dziga Vertov's "Man with a Camera," Kon described his work as "recording and composing continuously the manifestation of Tokyo as it is being made anew" (p. 7).

Contemporary everydayness is the receptacle of the "relic" and "ruin" for modern studies. These fragments of life being lived, like the surviving traces treasured by native ethnologists, were capable of disclosing the interior life of contemporaries by locating the social meaning they invested in them. Experience consisted of things "moving before the eye," always on the verge of escaping the gaze of the researcher, who had to seize this moving spectacle of the now in order to fix it momentarily, in other words, to grab hold of the present on the wing. Hence, the streets were like a vast "historical museum" pulsating with a constantly changing exhibition of things. As a result of this ongoing drama, the method of modernology demanded the researcher to "be there," or, as Kon put it, "standing inside the household, the closet, wandering among groups of modern girls, passing through public meeting places . . . we tend to forget the reality that becomes the stage which is our everyday life" (p. 8). With this insistence on the priority of immediate observation, Kon came close to making the urban ethnographer into a voyeur.

Kon's persistent emphasis on the importance of being there resembled Tosaka's identification of the *Da* (thereness) (*soko* in Japanese, even though he used the German). In Kon's world of the now, passing time was secondary to passing through space, where nothing was overlooked, not even the humblest cigarette butts thrown on the streets. Like Kracauer, Kon always fastened on what seemed to be the most trivial objects which, when spotted, he would sketch and then describe in detail. By the same measure, historical narrative was absent from Kon's recording of everyday life, even though his investigations demonstrated that the everyday was capable of vocalizing its own history. The content of his reports often exceeded the form itself, which provided both the impossible sense of immediacy (and the absence of mediation), best illustrated in his report on Inokashira Park on a warm afternoon, and fastened onto what he had openly admitted was unfastenable (for his illustration of the park and its visitors and an explanation of their activities, see pp. 28–32).

In this regard, the new documentary form of photography was better qualified to capture the moving present of everydayness and showed dramatically the point at which art and the everyday met, even though Kon preferred observing, interrogating, sketching, and supplying descriptive commentary. His reliance on almost artisanal methods to fix what otherwise could be better caught by the new photographic technology, especially the documentary form, indicates Kon's own ambivalence toward modernity and how, in effect, he was still relying on methods more appropriate to the conserving impulse of folkloric studies. While he believed a completed narrative preceded modernity, it was one (derived from Tarde) that marked three stages in the evolution to the present: (1) feudal custom, which was bad because only the rich were able to acquire things; (2) the nineteenth century, which made consumption accessible to all groups; and (3) modernity, during which people learned to approach consumption rationally. The first two stages of this scheme were the completed and forgotten historical antecedent to a moving present that now made its own history stretching into an indefinite future that would never be completed. In this sense, past was merely prehistory to an endless present indistinguishable from the future.

Finally, Kon regarded his discipline as a counterfoil to economic science. He hoped that *kōgengaku* would foster a subjective attitude that could persuade people not to buy useless goods and becoming entrapped by commodification and "economism."[18] He knew that modern economics was devoted to the "study of merchandising commodities . . . as exchange value, [whereas] modernology treats these things as useful objects." Paradoxically, though, he recognized that if fashion and fad (*ryūkō*) were associated with "wasteful things," they were still empowered to liberate people from the grip of feudal custom, tradition, and etiquette. In short, the "flair for fashion," as Benjamin called it, could liberate people from a feudalism ruled by fixed and unswerving custom and its notorious "disregard for everyday life" at the same time it imprisoned people in a new form of bondage. Feudalism excluded the possibility of everyday life (a view shared by Tosaka) because it was "unsubjective" and thus lacked the necessary "freedom" with which to determine the "forms of daily life." Living in a moment without the experience of what Kon called a "life revolution," locked in externalized modern forms that had not yet reached the interior life of the self, he appealed to the implementation of a modernization process aimed at socializing people into an "attitude toward everyday life" based on actually experiencing it.

While Kon's phenomenological investigations brought him into a close relationship to the details and commodities dominating modern everyday life, his method prevented him from looking beyond the surface to discover what lay under them. The meaning he claimed to have found in everyday consumption was simply a replay of his faith in a rationality that represented for him a decisive move away from the customary world of feudalism. Modern custom represented the regime of rationality and a social world that was dynamic and mobile rather than fixed and static. In other words, the method of modernology yielded only the most minute description of the details of everyday life, not the rationality he expected that would save the consumer from commodification and objectification. The world that Kon described as rational and efficient was being explained by his contemporary Aono Suekichi as unhappy, contradictory, and irrational. The past that Kon wished to discard seemed to return to the present, like a ghost, threatening reprisals and demanding retribution for the price of modernization.

In Germany, in his ethnographic report on the plight of the white-collar classes whose search for a "home" coincided with the economic and moral collapse of their world, Siegfried Kracauer alerted the country to the tenuous relationship between rationalization and the depletion of middle-class workers, between consumerist expectations and the consequences of capitalist crises. At precisely the same time, halfway around the globe in Japan, Aono Suekichi was publishing his *Sararīman kyōfu jidai*, and the title page of the "The Salaryman's Panic Time" portrayed a man falling to earth from a building.[19] Kracauer reported on the living conditions, attitudes, pleasures, and aspirations of the German white-collar class—the petite bourgeoisie—as they sank deeper into the mire of economic despair, comforted only by the fictions of "cultural goods" and yearning for the safety of "shelter" and a "return to home." Aono's work, however, more formally analyzed the social structure of the salaryman class (Japan's petite bourgeoisie) in the larger context of capitalist social relations in order to explain how and why they were fated to a life of continuing unhappiness and psychological depression caused by the growing disparity between their consumerist expectations and their inability to satisfy them. Aono's salarymen are the same people Kon Wajirō was investing with subjectivity as consumers who were in a position to know how to choose commodities for their specific utility. Both Kracauer and Aono, in contrast to Kon, identified this class with the process of rationalization that it had mastered but was now undermining its social and economic position in society.[20]

Aono saw the Japanese petite bourgeoisie crushed by the weight of "big capital," even though the social malaise he was reporting affected all groups in the present. Because the white-collar class occupied a position between the upper middle class and landowners, on the one hand, and the proletariat and tenant farmers, on the other, they experienced the worst of all "life lines." Economically, they shared with the laborer and farmer genuine hardships; socially, they stood with the upper bourgeoisie as cultural custodians. Despite their kinship with the laboring poor in the cities and the countryside, the petite bourgeoisie were conscious of the contradictory position they occupied in a way that had not yet been perceived by other classes. Worse, they still could not do anything about their particular plight. They were able neither to form an organization that could respond to social distress nor to find a position from which to produce the faintest sign of struggle that would announce the "dawn of emancipation" (Aono, p. 10).

For Aono, the panic time of the salaryman was nothing less than the prospect of mass starvation and the total "impoverishment of the spirit." By the same measure, he was convinced that the circumstances of spiritual impoverishment experienced by the petite bourgeoisie could be seen as a trope—"a miniaturized and signifying value"—pointing to a broader socially shared fate confronting

Japanese society. Grief, he argued, is a contemporary custom, a habit of social misery spreading throughout society but experienced most intensely by the white-collar class. What was important to understanding the contemporary custom of grief, as he put it, was comprehending the "lived experience" of people themselves in order to understand the "reality" and "direction" of this particular class. Although job insecurity terrorized the salarymen's everyday existence and reinforced the panic they collectively were experiencing, the main custom of hardship lay in the "spiritual and psychological precinct" and was signified by the "insufficiencies of materiality" in their lives (p. 24). In Aono's equation, spiritual distress emanated from specific psychological habits.

Although salarymen considered their social class to belonging to the bourgeoisie, they realized the impossibility of ever securing either "glory" and "honor" in politics and society commensurate with their position. Like workers, they were dissatisfied with both the conditions of their material life and a "frame of mind" that reminded them of their social inferiority. They aspired to living a tidy, correct, and peaceful existence, Aono observed, and psychologically, they liked to present themselves as composed, optimistic, serene, cheerful, peaceful, and harmonious, all habits, they believed, that were emblematic of their social location. While they actively repudiated the "reservoir of old morality," the customs of a feudal past, they nonetheless sought to preserve the ethics informing kin and familial relationships, neighborly associations, and friendships. In the salarymen's consciousness, Aono added, "there was the nature of the fields and gardens, the true circumstances of their parent's home, the obligation to relatives, and the relationship of friends." The calm, clear, and serene composure they desired originated not only from their valuation of harmony but also from the moral character of the class. In this way, the salarymen constituted both a progressive social stratum and an intellectual class. As an intelligentsia, they alone, paradoxically, had discovered the modern individualistic consciousness at the same time that they found themselves devoted to retaining older conceptions of ethical relationships. Perceiving this double bind as a contradiction that was the source of their hardship, their lives were flawed by alienation and a psychological habit of permanent dis-satisfaction. "The social reality lived by the salaryman has failed to satisfy their living and habits and their mental frame of mind." Although salarymen want to pursue a peaceful nature, what they get instead is a house barely in the suburbs with a garden that looks out only to the sky. When they try to lead an orderly and harmo-nious existence with relatives, they get the "icy separation of hus-band and wife, older brother and older sister." And while they want to comport themselves morally with their neighbors and friends, they receive only thoughtless hostility and competition. Their quest for a quietly moral and bright life was "betrayed," and "dis-illusionment" followed on "disillusionment." In the petite bour-geois household, the wife reinforced the atmosphere of "psycho-logical distress" by reminding her husband that his failures, rather than society at large, were the cause of his unhappiness. She avoided appealing to genuine social ills by attributing her hus-band's bad luck to his own incompetence and inadequacy. The present, Aono warned, was witnessing the first steps of a "familis-tic tragedy among the salaryman class'" (Aono, p. 24).

Only the petite bourgeoisie still seemed capable of maintain-ing the customary relations between husband and wife as the spir-itual basis of the family. The tragedy they were living came with their determination to retain the "love between husband and wife in the traditional sense as the spiritual basis of the family" at the moment the class was collapsing and the proletarian had aban-doned all meaning associated with the family because of poverty (p. 28). Aono explained that the "close proximity" to the bour-geoisie as the object of desire and imitation contributed immensely to the salarymen's plight. Yearning for this lifestyle and propelled by envy for the unobtainable, they found themselves reaching out for a life well beyond their reach. Even though the salarymen were produced by modern capitalism, the class paradoxically embraced values and attitudes often belonging to another time, which were made to coexist alongside more modern conduct and customs.

With this observation, Aono recognized the role of unevenness in the formation of modern Japanese society. It was not simply a role demanded by capitalism that divided city and countryside or even that accounted for the economic disparity between classes in the cities. Rather, this unevenness showed how the past interacted with a present that was constantly conjuring it. The coexistence of different values and customs signified different temporalities in the present within a single class and thus revealed a contradiction that had to be resolved. Aono's perception of the presence of an unevenness—rooted in the inherence of the past in the present, in which the everyday was the site of the ideological struggle over values—clashed with Kon's representation of an everydayness colonized by things that people consumed usefully to represent the triumph of a rationalization process that worked only to conceal contradictions and unevenness at the heart of lived experience. In this way, Aono asserted, "the tragedy of the salaryman is completely one of self-contradiction" that bonded the reality of a proletarianized life and bourgeois psychological ideals to feudal custom, "the contradiction between the modern individualistic pursuit and the quest for harmonious familism [of the past]" (p. 30).

Aono thus attributed the unhappiness caused by unevenness (the "panic") to the "commodity form" (*shohin ikko*) and the production of "knowledge" and the subsequent refinement of "technical skills" under capitalism, that is, the rationalization that had inspired Kon Wajirō to change the consumer into a knowing subject capable of making informed decisions on the basis of use value. Aono was less sure of the harmful effects of rationalization, which he seemed to identify with reification, inasmuch as he recognized that skills and knowledge, like anything else, could be bought and sold. Society, he observed, was producing new forms of knowledge and new skills that were being mastered by the salaryman class. But capitalism, he noted, had made no attempt to distinguish among commodities. In the calculations of the market, there was no real distinction between "shoes" and "knowledge," but only among units of quantity. To maintain price levels, it was often necessary to "burn" great quantities of commodities. When knowledge and skills became commodified, the difficulty was compounded because the salarymen who had mastered these skills were not commodities that could easily be discarded or destroyed to maintain market price. But they could always be fired from their jobs.

At one level, then, new skills and knowledge accelerated surplus production to end the problem of scarcity, but at another level, overproduction devalued market prices, which undermined the stability of secure employment and ultimately diminished its real value. The result of the "universalization and equalization" of skills and intelligence was the proliferation of competition for fewer jobs and the emergence of chronic "conflict among the social classes" for the guarantee of greater security. Moreover, the increasing conflict among the classes over scarce resources reawakened the "oppression of regressive elements," which referred to the reproduction of feudal practices to secure greater control and order despite the discontent and dissatisfaction among large numbers of people. Aono saw the renewal of feudal practices (as did Tosaka) in his present as a further intensification of the unevenness that already was being lived by the salarymen in their everyday lives. Unemployment and the concomitant contest for fewer jobs led to the "proletarianization" of the salarymen, who "descended to the gate of hell and passed through to reappear on the other side as an intellectual proletariat" (Aono, p. 39).

On the surface, the panic was manifest in the social customs and behavior of large numbers of people who belonged to the petite bourgeois class. The panic they felt and dreaded appeared as the "modern decadence circulating throughout the cities, in its jazz joints, dance halls, and cafes" and in the proliferation and spread of a new style of sexual conduct, called collectively "nonsense eroticism," a world of frenzy (*kyōsō*) and bewilderment (*wakuran*). "The living things that danced furiously and madly," Aono reported, "were hopeless petite bourgeoisie — the salaryman class. Originally, modern dance seemed to offer endless variety." But in time, the common psychological attraction that drew throngs of people to dance halls promised to satisfy the "quest to evade or overcome reality propelled by the demand for antireality." In Aono's reckoning, the social customs enacted by the panic-stricken petite bourgeoisie represented a mysterious social hieroglyphic concealing a deeper reality lived and experienced. People flocked to dance halls and danced wildly out of a panic stemming from the "darkness of reality," the "shivering" provoked by reality, and they soon realized that it was "hopeless to live within the present by trying to make it a step-ping-stone to reality" (Aono, p. 41). The madness of dance, the paralysis produced by excessive alcohol consumption, and the uproar caused by the jazz took from people both their reason and their means to control themselves. But the frenzied activity also revealed rage and resentment that "bulged" with anger. Aono recorded the same kind of resentment accumulated by the German petite bourgeoisie that Ernst Bloch observed in the early 1930s and what he — Bloch — described as an internal and subjective "muffled nondesire for the Now . . . noncontemporaneous," "an impoverished center," "spiritually missed."[21]

The tragedy of the Japanese salarymen was generated by overdetermined contradictions that placed them in the anomalous role of intellectual producers whose skills and value were being undermined by the market, as guardians of a specific cultural endowment that the modern present was increasingly discounting. The psychological despair that resulted from experiencing both a diminution of their social position and the disappearance of the culture they had once cherished contributed to their spiritual "emptying out." Because they occupied a subordinate position in the social economy, the salarymen's "spiritual and psychological consciousness" was subject to that of the ruling class, which meant they still lacked a strong, autonomous spiritual life.

Under these circumstances, Aono's appeal to the centrality of spiritual life now absent from the petite bourgeoisie conveyed the associations of culture that in the 1920s had already become identified with the domain of spirit (*seishin*), the world of nonmaterial values. Even though the class seemed to sink lower on the economic scale, it could not easily change its psychology and consciousness. Aono located the philosophic basis of the salaryman's "worldview" in conservative "idealism" and the aspirations for a lifestyle equal to that of the upper bourgeoisie. This view presupposed that "spirit," "spiritualism," "consciousness," and the "we" decided all things, that even "history," "society," the "state" and "this world were determined by the spiritual thing"(Aono, p. 87). Although he recognized that this idealistic worldview did not participate directly in the productive process, because it was the "philosophy of the leisure class," it was at the heart of the salaryman's cultural and spiritual life and the basis on which all things were judged. Idealist philosophy was marked by the absence of dialectics (p. 88) and thus privileged nonmovement, stasis, and the stilling and fixing of things and managed to uphold a consciousness that "saw nothing in the eye," like the "world," "society," and the "state."

Once this philosophy entered the worldview of the salaryman, it was immediately made contiguous to the now time of the everyday present, which it read as a contradiction. This juxtaposition signaled the particular moment at which culture itself was polarized into two registers, between a high, spiritual level and a low, popular, material, and vulgar one. In this new cultural economy, high meant fixed, still, unmoving (antihistorical), and eternal, and low referred to everydayness, the popular and vulgar worldview of the ever-new in the ever-same, world of the commodity and mass consumption.[22] Philosophy was given the task of explaining a true or truer experience, an authentic movement unaffected by the contingencies of history and change, a life of transcendent value, as opposed to one that was increasingly being lived and experienced by large numbers of people in the everyday of the industrialized cities. This was, of course, a life dominated by the commodity form, standardized, averaged, and homogenized, the denaturing of life in society. Philosophy sought not to analyze the social formation of the present — capitalism — but to supply cultural consolation against the onslaught of the commodity. Philosophic discourse thus sanctioned the separation of politics and culture, past and present, and ethics and aesthetics. It attempted to do this by inverting the life of the masses for the poetic, mythic, even the world of the natural nonbeing or nothingness, in which memory is less a product of lived experience in history than "accumulated and frequently unconscious data."[23]

It was this problem of philosophy and its commitment to cultural conceit that Tosaka Jun undertook to disassemble in his penetrating analysis of the Japanese ideology in 1935. In "Essays on the Japanese Ideology" (Nihon ideorogiron), Tosaka, with devastating logic, showed the utter bankruptcy of idealistic philosophical claims that projected the superiority of spirit and culture over considerations of history and political economy. It was for this reason that he sought to redefine the task of philosophy as the problem of the present, the now (*ima*) of everyday life. In contrast to Kon Wajirō, whom Tosaka considered to be a captive of the phenomenological objects of the everyday life he was investigating, the task of philosophy for Tosaka was to explain the everyday of the present in its totality because thought itself had been "quotidianized." While contemporary philosophy was hurriedly deployed to restore the regime of cultural spirit and to show how the essentials of Japan's cultural endowment had remained unchanged since the Stone Age, Tosaka was advising his contemporaries to consider the everyday as a central philosophical concept requiring elucidation.

Recalling the later example of Henri Lefebvre after World War II, Tosaka saw everyday life as the basic unifying element of the present, even though thinkers inside and outside Japan were insisting on its separation from philosophy. Philosophy had become too abstract, especially its idealistic inflection, too removed from everyday life when, in fact, it was precisely the concreteness of everydayness that offered philosophy a grounding for speculation and a new purpose. In Lefebvre's later articulation, everyday life served as a philosophical concept that could not be understood outside philosophy, thus qualifying it as its principal vocation.[24] For Tosaka, however, the problem appeared to be that philosophers were separated from the "actualities" of everyday life by their confusing metaphysics with reality. But philosophy today, he wrote, "is becoming properly everyday, like the phenomena we are talking about." Philosophy has been brought down to the world of common sense, to everyday life as it is being lived.[25]

What drove Tosaka—and contemporaries like Gonda Yasunosuke and Tsuchida Kyōson—in this project to reunite philosophy and everyday life was the desire to juxtapose an alternative everydayness and the production of modern custom to the fictive abstractions of national culture circulating in the 1930s. But their endeavor was also prompted by their sense of a forgotten and repressed history that had upheld the materiality of everyday life as the irreducible unit for all spatial configurations that the pre-Socratics, according to Tosaka, had first identified as the true vocation of philosophy. It was for this reason that Tosaka recommended accepting an "actual social life," as he put it, which meant engaging the immediately experienced of the performative present rather than following the givenness of a phenomenological perspective that sanctioned things as they were. It was here, too, that he seemed to reject the powerful claims of historical narrative—currently being produced by the contemporary Marxian debate over the nature of the development of capitalism in Japan—for a view of history written by the space of everyday life.

Three related considerations characterize Tosaka's discourse: (1) His response to the crisis of modernity stemmed from his conviction that "experience" was no longer being communicated adequately by received forms. What he meant was that custom (fūzoku) no longer reflected the conditions that produced it and the morality it was supposed to embody because it had hardened into convention. It is important to note that Tosaka was concentrating on the status of custom which, in his day, had acquired an almost iconic sense of timelessness. (2) By concentrating on everydayness, philosophy would be liberated from its dependence on religion, otherworldliness, and its celebration of the non-everyday. (3) Everydayness was primarily a spatial rather than a temporal category, since its temporality was structured by materiality always embodied by space. Here Tosaka revealed more than a hint of reliance on Heidegger and Watsuji Tetsurō's reading of Sein und Zeit and the emphasis placed on thereness. This Tosaka called the Da character of everyday life, not as an idea for the existent—the person who exists—but as an idea pointing to the character of spatial existence itself as the condition of existentiality resulting in the transposition of Being and temporality into everydayness and spatiality. With this move, Tosaka hoped to avoid the subjectivity of Heidegger's Dasein by positioning in the foreground the objectivity of "everyday-like space" (nichijōsei kūkan). As a consequence, temporality and the principles of history were subordinated to and structured by the everyday space of the now.

In a long essay on the relationship between custom and morality, Tosaka condemned any philosophy that was not properly concerned with "clothes." That is, clothing was merely one among many customs that people took for granted but was, in fact, the agency of "actuality." Custom, he asserted, "is from the beginning a certain mass phenomenon." But contemporary society conducted its affairs as if it had no need to connect custom to the people who make custom and live according to its constraints. Concern for the status of custom entailed showing an awareness of and sensitivity to the masses, since the production of custom and its role in determining conduct signified a common consent, the force of a recognized consensuality. Like Gramsci, Tosaka in his *Nihon ideorogiron* called this mass acquiescence to custom "common sense" whose effectiveness depended on its capacity to conceal its conditions of production behind the claims of natural averaging. This does not mean that Tosaka rejected the power of common sense but only the need to question its naturalist claims historically in order to construct a new consensus.

In his discussion of the status of custom, Tosaka appealed to Thomas Carlyle's *Sarter resartus* and asked why philosophy had been so indifferent to the most common things. Carlyle sensitized him to the significance of the mundane things of life rather than the merely transcendental and taught him the social importance of clothes, which he saw as a custom like any other, which needed to be understood theoretically in order to find out how and under which conditions a custom is produced. It is, moreover, the popular, the common, that is so often misunderstood and missed by philosophy. Yet the commonness of custom, however deceptive, is produced by the basic structure of society and its people and bears the imprint of this act of production. The substance of society "acquires skin, flesh, beautiful, or unsightly that is expressed in what we call custom; it ends in clothing."[26] Clothing functioned as a covering concealing the body that gave it shape, just as custom conceals the structure of society. Custom is society's physiognomy, its visage (recalling Walter Benjamin's identification of dates as the physiognomy of history). It possesses concreteness and embodiment which, if interrogated, will reveal the informing modes of productive labor implicated in social construction. By the same measure, it deceives because it presents an abstract side that makes custom appear autonomous, disembodied, and timeless.

Bourgeois social science has substituted the symptom or the sign of custom for its substance, masking the social conditions that have produced it but that it now conceals and mistakes it for the object of scientific inquiry. Here Tosaka called attention to Kon Wajirō's *kōgengaku* as a discipline committed to concealment and accepting custom and things as they appear rather than looking behind the mask for the historical and social conditions of production. Newspapers were even worse, he warned, easily skimming the surface, managing only to grasp custom at its most superficial and "unsteady" level, and giving the impression of something insubstantial. Because custom has been seen as autonomous, vulgar, and popular, it has not been seen as a social problem but only as a habit, the status quo, or common sense, and philosophy has been diverted to look elsewhere for its truths.

Tosaka argued that everyday life was identified with custom, which philosophers had discounted as a serious category for reflection, appealing instead to the "transcustomary" and transcendental to avoid the baseness and vulgarity that the common and mundane signified. The paradox of modern society is that it dismisses custom as "scornful" but refuses to see it as a social problem. The best example of this antimony is reflected in the question of contemporary sexuality. For Tosaka, living in a time that critics had already described as "grotesque," "erotic," and "nonsensical," sexual practices represented an instance of contemporary custom. In recent days, he wrote, women have apparently resorted to sexuality as "a support of individual existence," referring to both women's new independence working in the pleasure industry (cafes, bars, restaurants) and the obvious fact already reported by social researchers that large numbers of women had been brought to the cities to serve as prostitutes. By refusing to see this phenomenon as something more than a contemporary custom, society had failed to understand the incidence of prostitution as a major problem.

Unlike researchers like Kagawa Toyohiko, Tosaka was not calling attention simply to the moral dimensions of the sex industry and expressing outrage but, rather, to the reason that women at this particular moment in Japan's history were being recruited in such large numbers to satisfy the needs of the large cities' pleasure quarters. The women's problem, he charged, is completely ignored by relegating it to an attitude that encourages men to see women only as beauties who are "objects of teasing and pleasure." Tosaka was concerned with showing that custom is always rooted in the particular conditions that have produced it, in this instance, capitalism, and that it is related to the formation of morality. Rather than learning how contemporary sexuality became a custom, a common sense, it has been dismissed by concerned opinion as a question of what is morally correct or incorrect. (Tosaka was clearly criticizing the important statistical survey by Kagawa Toyohiko and Ando Nobuyoshi—"A Statistical Survey of Japanese Morality"— that represented the kind of social science that skimmed the surface by resorting to quantitative measures but condemned the practice under investigation by invoking a moral norm that had nothing to do with producing the phenomenon and which clearly displaced the real causes.) Morality supplies an index of political opinion, however, which is why it is important to pay close attention to how reality—"situatedness"—manages to make sexuality into the content of popular morality.

For Tosaka, linking custom to morality revealed a reality that reflected social authority—the claim to determine authoritatively what is proper or improper for society. The point he wished to make, as he did in his long meditations on common sense, was that the mere givenness of custom and morality escaped scientific and theoretical evaluation to project a transclass, transcendent perspective, secure in its timelessness and permanence, safely above all interest. Even though the sale of brides in Japan has been proclaimed unethical, he pointed out, contemporary practices relating to prostitution have escaped comparable judgment, principally because they were serving various business interests. To grasp custom in its situatedness and its condition of possibility would, he believed, go a long way to relieving society of its principal defects (*TJS*, p. 9).

What Tosaka looked for was a method that would locate the place of custom and morality, which meant its grounding in

productive relationships and discovering its subsequent ideolo-
gization according to a specific history and its class-based interest
(TJS, p. 13). The recognition of everyday life as the site of new
practices that defied convention rather than serving as the receptacle of timeless custom and morality put into question the claims
of timelessness. Custom was simply the shell, the outer garment
that concealed the kernel of morality (and authority) that authorized it. Its substance, even though it appeared to be abstract and
formal, a proper interrogation would bring to the surface. This
outer "skin," as Tosaka called it, granted morality an immunity
from scientific inquiry and authorized its claims to naturalness and
permanence. History was evacuated from custom, which was its
most powerful function, and this de-historicizing operation worked
to remove both custom and morality as social problems worthy of
investigation. In the hands of folklorists, dehistoricizing custom
became the principal condition of preserving it. The very reason
prompting the neglect of analyzing custom philosophically
explains why everyday life itself escaped serious attention.

     "If the purpose today is to consider otherworldly things, it will
mark the special feature of . . . worldly things. People start talking
expressly like that because they see conditions that cause them to
employ such contrary Buddhist beliefs to the widespread vulgarity
[they perceive] in this time of the present." Tosaka was responding
to the observation that the "one modern philosophical term that has
been understood most vulgarly has been the word for everyday life"
(TJZ 3:136). To see the everyday life as vulgar and base is to judge
its unwanted presence in the present as a decline from an original,
higher form of existence. This view, pointing to the Heideggerian
dismissal of the inauthentic everyday life, was especially common
among those who lived an "original religious life." But these lives
are separate from the masses who inhabit everyday life. "Those who
do not believe in everydayness are mainly religious people in the
widest sense of the word" (p. 136). Talking about an other world is
the subject of theology, not philosophy.

     Calling to mind his earlier program to see custom as a cate-
gory that should be analyzed fully, Tosaka discounted the theo-
logical disregard for daily life by proposing that the existence of an

other world signified the abstract, which stood in contrast to the concreteness offered by everyday life. Theologians, whom he described as "philosophers of the other world," invariably misrecognized the special character of everydayness in its relationship to the people. Only when theology was incorporated into philosophy would it be reunited with the human. Like Benjamin, Tosaka saw the experience of everydayness as the proper substitute for religion.

Everyday life follows a pattern of repetition reflected in the cycle of loving, planning, and reflection; it is both material and concrete (*TJZ*, p. 137). The materiality of the commonplace, in which practices are repeated, is never completed, always constitutes a partial historicization, and stands in opposition to the lofty and the profound world beyond custom that is premised on fullness and completion. Tosaka's vision of everydayness offered a realm of imminence, as contrasted to a world that put life outside and beyond human reach. Contemporary philosophy has tried to finesse this distinction by employing the term *genjitsu* (reality) to describe the non-everyday world of metaphysics. The term, he reasoned, encompassed the concrete abstractly as mere appearance, but at the same time, it transformed reality into the "unreal" and even a "false reality."

According to the conception of reality embraced by the "apostles" of "will," "subjectivity," or the "personal," the false concrete is what characterizes everyday existence. In place of using *genjitsu*, Tosaka preferred the word *actuality* (in *romaji*) to describe the rules of daily life (*TJZ*, p. 137). Even though this term had been used in metaphysics and as recently as by the Italian philosopher of fascism Giovanni Gentile, Tosaka hoped he might avoid these "idealistic" dangers by showing how "actuality" was linked to facticity, temporality, and space. If the most common event is freed from metaphysics and submitted to a philosophical consideration that takes into account its history, everyday life will be liberated from convention and necessity and opened to possibility. What is important is relating everyday life to the current situation (*genjō bunseki*). "When talking about daily occurrences, what is more important in the life of the masses than whether or not there will be enough rice and tea?" Discrimination of the nature of the current situation will save philosophy from its habitual dependence on abstraction, which might be a "hobby" for "deep philosophers" and "literary men, like salarymen chanting noh." But the purpose of uniting philosophy with the current situation is to explain the "material character of existence" (*TJZ* 3:71) and thus recognize its true vocation as a critical practice. In this regard, philosophy can learn something from journalism which is, at its best, criticism of everyday life. Only criticism that begins with the current situation and contemporary events can offer the "best defense against a metaphysics of interpretation" that produces the principle of criticism but not the critical act (*TJZ* 3:140).

Finally, Tosaka, like Kon, identified everydayness as the "today"—and, still more, the "now"—that shared the same structure as the present (*gendai*) and contemporaneity. This sense of nowness—the space of everyday life—produces the actual, consisting of the principles of daily existence, and is the place where actualization is carried out. When historical time is seen to be determined by these principles of everydayness, which constitute the "mystery of history," the everyday life is reunited with history inasmuch as it is recognized as the space that conceals or "shelters" the "kernel of the crystal of historical time." Tosaka pointed to the reduction of the seemingly endless flow of historical time to the most basic and minimal unit of existence, the day-to-day interaction structuring experience. In his view, living is always in the present, properly in the contemporary (*gendai*), "in a period named the present." At the same time, a "today" that epitomizes the present age and shares with it the principle of meaning is the "principle of everydayness." Hence, historical time is governed by the principle of everyday life as it is lived. The present is "miniaturized" in the today (*konnichi*) and even more in the temporality of the "now" (*ima*). The temporality of the now functions metonymically to disclose the nature of the present, contemporary reality that it shares.

Tosaka's conception of the everyday represented a routine and repetitive unfolding of successive days held together by common occurrences yet able to be differentiated from one another. It was this difference that the everyday concealed or "sheltered" and that formed the mystery of history, the principle of an absolute, inescapable everyday life that "shelter[ed] the crystal of the kernel of historical time." This phrase referred to a conviction that in the repetition of daily routine, the criticism of custom would reveal new possibilities for changing convention.

Rather than recognizing death in the future as the moment structuring life, as envisaged by Heidegger, Tosaka appealed to the idea of work, work time limited by one's death. This stemmed from his belief that the thereness of everyday life preceded the presence of Being and that it was labor that reproduced its space. Because "death's time comes," it is necessary to put work into order within a fixed time frame. Days accumulate in succession, but today and tomorrow are not interchangeable. The perspective of the present, the now, is always the time of work, not tomorrow, which may never come because of death. In this way, Tosaka insisted, the today, the now, has a "solidity," and practice must conform to its immediate situation, its historical moment. Temporality was thus cast into the space of everyday life, determined by its "thereness," just as Tosaka's contemporary the linguist Tokieda Motoki was envisioning what he called the "scene" (*bamen*) of speaking that would supply the referent to language usage. This *Da*-ness signi-fied a materiality, an "anywhere," "locus," "situation," determined by extension, continuity, succession, and length. In this space, humans manage their practical activity according to matter within a presentness (*ima*)—the now—and its repetition rather than the dictates of a destiny from the future (*TJZ* 3:264). For Tosaka every-dayness always returned to materiality.

In other words, Tosaka saw everydayness as a space contain-ing material properties identified by their *Da* character. The qual-ity of thereness was reserved for everyday space rather than the Hei-deggerian Being. It was this conception of everyday space that the cinema director Ozu Yasujirō captured in a number of postwar films presenting the autonomy of everyday life in frames devoid of character or movement as the "site of reproductive nostalgia,"[27] its sheer materiality rather than the Deleuzian "banality" of ordinary things. Moreover, this space structured the temporality of those who inhabited it according to the succession of days that preceded and followed the now—today. For Tosaka, unlike Heidegger, the today was the present, the place of custom and repeated activities, an always uncompleted historicization that would itself defy the claims of historical narrative as the space of actualization. The kernel of history lay in this sedimented everydayness and would be disclosed when criticism of custom and morality made available new possibilities. In this sense, the identity of history was the difference that actualization produced from the sedimented layers of todays and yesterdays. Although it is not difficult to guess just what these possibilities entailed, Tosaka stopped short of spelling them out in programmatic detail, owing to censorship and the threat of state repression. We know that he counted planning as one of the main activities of everyday life, and in his prescient text "The Principles of Everydayness and Historical Time," he conceded that historical periodization reflected the importance of politics in establishing eras. Significant moments or periods possessed a distinct and dominant characteristic that was always produced by politics. Clearly, criticism of custom in everyday life—actualizing the givenness of the present—pointed to possible political paths leading to what he saw as the "creation of new conventions."

Like so many in Japan between the wars, Tosaka's image of everydayness appeared to consist of a sedimentation of myriad practices, its temporality derived from the succession of days, yesterday, today, and tomorrow, or a layering of successive nows. But he was also sensitive to the promise of contingent happenings, chance occurrences, unexpected meetings, and surprising events which, if properly and critically analyzed—actualized—could lead to the destruction of conventions as well as to the refiguration of their meaning by more explicit forms of intervention producing new conventions and custom.

Tosaka worked formally within the framework of a philosophical discourse devoted to the study of materialism, much like his great Italian contemporary Antonio Gramsci, who coded Marxism as a philosophy of praxis. It was the logic of this discourse that opened the way to thinking about how everyday practices might be disrupted, not the appeal to an explicit theory of revolution constituting a nodal event in the progression of a fictive narrative. This was the function of criticism in Tosaka's thinking. Yet as a Marxist, he still insisted on the importance of class and world history. "It is inadequate if the individual who is an I or society is not seen as a member of a class, if one day is not recognized as one in world history." His conception of the everyday, which was located "anywhere," immediately called attention to the relationship between the singular and local and the general and global. This was as true of Japan as it was any other society experiencing the routines and repetitions of everyday life under capitalism. But it was also true that within this space there were other possibilities. Everydayness was the place and time for countless practices that could, through the agency of critique—actualization—overturn received conventions to mark the difference between yesterday and today. Like Lefebvre, Tosaka saw the everyday as the intersection of repetitions and the place that was always ready for the practice of criticism which, he hoped, writing only a few years before his imprisonment and death, would give philosophy its final meaning by returning it to the material conditions and practical existence that had originally given it life (*TJZ* 3:162).

The critic Kobayashi Hideo could agree with Tosaka that thought was nothing if it was not informed by practical life. He could also agree that literature, not history or ethnography, was the principal site for the expression of everyday common sense. But Kobayashi also acknowledged that Tosaka and he were different kinds of realists. While both believed that the novel was the form that best communicated the experience of everyday life as it was being lived in Japan, they differed over which kind of novel best performed this function. For Kobayashi, this role was occupied by the *shishōsetsu*—a hybrid form developed in twentieth-century Japan to convey the experience of living in a time of rapid transformation and still retaining elements of an older literary tradition. The controversy was over the claims of what was called a "pure literature" that concentrated on the solitary self—seemingly removed from society—and the novel of proletarian realism that was to serve the class struggle. Yet Kobayashi was, I believe, more right than wrong in this argument, because the I novel attested to its embeddedness in a specific everyday life that spoke of the social and historical temporality of Japan that would have been recognizable to Tosaka. In fact, Kobayashi observed, "Marxist writers have rejected the mundane" as material for fiction. "It was not that young Marxists had lost the feel for everyday life," he continued, "but that their ideology instructed them to transform the concept of 'life' from the mundane to the historical."[28] In his 1930s essay "Thought and Real Life" (Shisō to jiseikatsu), he proposed that there is no worthwhile thought that is separate from real life. "A thought that fails to pursue making sacrifice in real life is lodged only in the head of animals. Social order is nothing more than the sacrifice that real life pays in thought. . . . nurtured by the customary sacrifice of real life."[29]

For Kobayashi, the contemporary writer who best exemplified the relationship between thought and everyday life was Shiga Naoya, even though he was willing to praise others like Kikuchi Kan as practitioners of everyday culture. "Shiga," Kobayashi wrote,

> was a man of action, who had the spirit of a man of deeds. The skills he possessed would have no meaning if separated from the real. In Shiga, it is natural that what he produced was absorbed in real life, as part of everyday life. Art does not appear according to the dissolution of real life. (KHS, p. 231)

No writer, he added, was more devoted to transmuting theories of everyday life into art. It was precisely because literature was better able to communicate the experience of everyday life—the concreteness from which it was figured—that it was a more superior form than historical narrative, which he saw sliding into unrelieved abstraction and forgetfulness. In this regard, Tosaka Jun's conception of a historical temporality driven by the principles of everydayness came close to Kobayashi's own rejection of historical narratives. With Kobayashi, the I novel appeared as a quintessential act of memoration.

In "History and Literature," written just before the beginning of the war, Kobayashi claimed that historical narrative had lost its living relationship to the present-real life. As a form, it could no longer convey memory and thus stood as the sign for modern forgetting by imaging the present as the culmination of progress. He wanted to show that history never repeated itself, as historians believed, and that its claim to represent the narrative of progressive development fixed firmly a fiction of almost unmanageable proportions. It is important to suggest that although Kobayashi disliked the practice of historiography, he did value the past. In accounting for the development leading to a progressive present, history has had to rely on a closed causal chain that excludes and omits personal and common experiences like loss and a memory of the past. Modernity demands forgetting and thus forfeits the possibility of realizing memorative communication, which only literature can rescue. What is forgotten is particularly the everyday that Blanchot much later pointed out "we cannot help but miss" because it is not yet "information."[30] If, for example, the attitude of a mother whose child has died is considered, the historical reality of the event will be different from how it was experienced. Historical reality would stop with a consideration of causes and conditions. In the process, though, the meaning will be lost if the event, the loss of a child, is not accompanied by emotion. And if sentiment and feeling are not expressed, there is no reason for the figure of the infant "to flicker before the [mind's] eye" as a memory-image, even though the occurrence of death is explained in detail. What Kobayashi hoped to emphasize with this example was his conviction that historical reality was always incomplete because it recorded only the existence of the event. The mother knows this lesson, he remarked, and she knows that the death of the child will fail to qualify as historical reality unless it is also invested with genuine feeling.

Meaning comes not from the event as such but from those who feel its force, which strangely becomes an event to be remembered. The love of the mother is the source of this meaning, and the child continues to exist because she still loves it "today," long after it has died. For this reason alone, it is not necessary to appeal to the details surrounding the cause of death in order to remember the child in the heart. In the mother's thinking, the facts are not reliable or necessary for restoring the memory of the child. Kobayashi complained that the easy invocation of historical concreteness and objectivity made by contemporary historians attests only to vagueness and abstraction. But if historians insist on continuing to use such terms to explain history, then the mother's response is a better example of actualizing historical reality, concretizing it, and making it objective. These things experienced everyday, he believed in his "gut," are what really constitute history and are generally omitted from historical reality. "Are we being paradoxical," he asked, "when we talk about things experienced in daily life?"

Acknowledging that he was no philosopher, Kobayashi was still convinced that the "wisdom related to the history that we experience intuitively is not deformed or misshapen [*fugu*]" (*KHS*, p. 277). In fact, the mother, who is not a trained historian, uses the historian's techniques more skillfully to "breathe" memory into a history closer to her life. Everyday life is thus both the site of experience whose meaning is supplied by those who lived it and the reservoir of memory that historical narrative must forget in the interest of communicating reason. Contemporary man, he charged, "sits astride a dumb horse called the rational development of history and whips it while screaming freedom and progress; the dumb horse ought to know the distinction" (p. 278). Kobayashi, who could not have read Benjamin, described the pursuit of civilization as a "barbaric quest." Historical practice resembled a large bamboo basket that scoops up from the "great sea of history" nothing more than minnows. History misses the vast spectacle of human existence taking place before its eyes. Appealing to a text from Japan's medieval period, the *Heike monogatari*, Kobayashi explained that while the author was also concerned with development, it was felt like a weight on his body. The author personally shouldered, so to speak, the weight of a contingent history. The representation of his feelings was essential to what was being recorded. Contemporaries find the contingent and "unreasonable" in history to be inconvenient, since only progress is necessary and favorable. Causal relationships that the brain invents to tell this story have nothing to do with the experience close to everyday life that creates fresh historical emotions in the heart. "I experience the necessity of history only where freedom and contingency have been crushed" (p. 280). In this sense, Kobayashi invested everydayness with the power to imagine and recall, as opposed to a history driven by reason and the will to forget.

History, Kobayashi concluded, is a "classic," a mirror of the self that constantly needs to be polished by the poet's intuitive power. Invoking the figure of the fourteenth-century loyalist historian Kitabatake Chikafusa, he explained that his historical view never moves because it stems from the experiences of everyday life. Literature showed that history occupies a place that never moves—what he called the "mystery of the place that never moves"—which teaches us that theories of historical change are no longer necessary. What Kobayashi meant by referring to history as motionless mystery was that it was like the everyday that never changed. This was the place of "disquiet" the Portuguese poet Fernando Pessoa identified that was missing from history, the innumerable common occurrences of daily life that remained opened to Kobayashi, reading Kitabatake, when it was necessary to repeat the act of "polishing the soul's mirror" not for acquiring knowledge but for restoring the spirit (*KHS*, p. 289). It was this commonness of experience lived in the everyday—history's disquiet—in which history appears motionless and as the sign of a common tradition of emotional life derived from everyday life, which remained the same yet always was open to the necessity of "polishing the mirror." But in the end, Kobayashi managed only to remystify everyday life, making it impenetrable to all but a few, like poets and artists who could understand the "mystery of the place that never moves" that required recognizing the commonness of feeling and emotion. By reidentifying everydayness as the site of aura, he risked arriving at the same place contemporary fascist theorists had already reached.

Whereas Tosaka Jun saw everydayness "anywhere" linked to the larger processes of world history, Kobayashi was convinced that he saw in it a new historical conception for a Japan desperately seeking to overcome the modern. What momentarily appeared to link the historical present to the future, the local to the global, turned back on itself to transform the particular into the exceptional, the present into the past, everydayness into eternal values of feeling that create art. It is important to note that Kobayashi's privileging of the common experience of everydayness not only destroyed the distinction between past and present, making the present the past, but it also made possible the separation of everyday life from the critique that Tosaka had designated as the philosophical vocation of the now. In this regard, the possibility of joining everydayness to political practice was aborted with Tosaka's death and seemingly foreclosed for the future. Postwar Japan, which Tosaka never lived to see but which Kobayashi experienced until 1970, made a few feeble attempts to link everyday life and politics, that is, democracy. But it quickly veered off toward establishing one-party rule and displacing political participation with policies calling for "high economic growth" and "income doubling" and toward recovering the missed spirit of an eternal life that had remained unchanged since the beginning of time.

In many ways, Kobayashi Hideo's postwar masterpiece, *Motoori Norinaga*, supplied the terms and argument for eternalizing a native aesthetic endowment that had miraculously managed to exceed history itself. Such a society would be better served by the idea of culture prefigured in Kobayashi's conception of everyday life, whose celebration of eternal core values that transcend past and present and privilege cultural value over formation reinforced an arrangement separating everyday life from history, custom from its conditions of production, aesthetics from ethics, leaving it only with consumption rather than the possibility of actualizing critique in the interest of realizing a genuinely participatory democracy. In postwar Japan, only the films of Ozu Yasujirō recall for us both the temporality of that moment when everyday life promised new possibilities and its customary materiality that granted it autonomy. These films look back to an everydayness that in the 1950s was already disappearing and being replaced by a new conception of a society fashioned as a postwar order. Still, in the work called *gutai* (concrete) of the performative artists of the 1950s and 1960s, perhaps we have a momentary reminder of an effort to reenvisage an everydayness rooted in the concreteness of lived experience. The work of the *gutai* group prefigured later forms of artistic performance that sought, perhaps heroically, to find new modes of practice with which to construct a critique of society that seemed to have ended with the struggle over the U.S.-Japan Security Pact and the failure to prevent the return of a state that wanted only to be an improved version of its prewar predecessor.

If the performance art of the *gutai* group sought to resituate the concrete in postwar Japanese life, the director Imamura Shohei provided an example of a possible history written by the everyday in his extraordinary documentary *History of Postwar Japan as Told by a Barmaid*. In this brilliant deployment of the documentary form, reminiscent of possibilities associated with the earlier discovery of everydayness before the war, Imamura tried to lay hold of a history of the present—the immediate postwar years—as lived and experienced by his interlocutor, Onboro, who gradually shows that her everyday life reveals a history sharply different from the publicly evolving narrative of political events marking Japan's recovery in the 1950s and 1960s. The scene of the postwar, then, opens on a vast site of unevenness in which different histories are being lived. What the director succeeds in orchestrating is the coexistence of different narratives and temporalities—especially the experience of everyday life writing its own history and thus marking a radical difference against the backdrop of publicly developing events relating to the official political history of postwar Japan. Imamura's barmaid is mercifully free from the structure of repetitive disavowal that represents Japan as successfully modern at the same time it portrays Japanese as essentially unchanged, as if the latter were incommensurate to the former. Moreover, the decision to use film and the form of the documentary contrasts with Kon Wajirō's more artisanal choice to supply his own drawings and Kobayashi's designation of the novelistic form to grasp the details of everyday life.

With Imamura, the film documentary becomes the proper mode for immersion into everyday life, standing in immediate contrast to the ongoing public narrative that punctuates the bar maiden's experience that is more written than seen, even though filmed it will become the official version of postwar history. Imamura shows that for the barmaid everyday life—shadowed by the glare of public events—is where the ideological struggles over value are fought and where an open ended and incomplete present, contradictory yet multi-accentual, writes its history of difference. As

Imamura demonstrates, this history of the present and its difference has nothing to do with the fetishized object of revenance Japan's modernity has incessantly called forth to signify its difference. Imamura's barmaid understands what Pessoa's Soares felt when, more than thirty years earlier, he confessed his anguish at feeling a "disquiet" simply over "being here," a nostalgia for something "never known," and a modernity that deep down "is so ancient, hidden, so different from the meaning that shines out from all this."

Introduction: The Unavoidable "Actuality" of Everyday Life

1. Fernando Pessoa, *The Book of Disquiet,* ed. Maria Jose du Lancastre and trans. Margaret Jull Costa (London: Serpent's Tail, 1991), p. 5. Cited in the text as Pessoa.

2. Françoise Proust, *L'Histoire á contretemps* (Paris: Les éditions du Cerf, 1994), pp. 13, 15.

3. Ibid., p.15.

4. John Roberts, *The Art of Interruption* (Manchester: Manchester University Press, 1998), p.12. Roberts has described the everyday as a trope.

5. See David Landes, *The Wealth and Poverty of Nations* (Boston: Abacus, 1997), p. 363.

6. Peter Novick, *That Noble Dream: The "Objectivity Question" and the American Historical Profession* (Cambridge: Cambridge University Press, 1988).

7. Gendai Nihon shisō taikei, *Yanagita Kunio,* ed. Masada Katsumi (Tokyo: Chikuma shobō, 1965), pp. 283–284.

8. Richard Evans, *In Defense of History* (New York: Norton, 1999).

9. See, by all means, V. V. Voloshinov's penetrating and overlooked critique of philology in his *Marxism and the Philosophy of Language,* trans. L. Majeska and I. R. Titunik (New York: Seminar Press, 1973). This work, written in the 1920s, already recognized that the study of linguistics was based on the "concern with cadavers of written languages" (pp. 71–73). The same could be said of the Rankean model of history.

10. Evans, *In Defense of History,* p. 82, quoting Laurence Stone.

11. Proust, *L'Histoire,* p.13.

12. Benedict Anderson, *The Specter of Comparison* (London: Verso, 1998), p. 2.

13. Proust, *L'Histoire,* p. 10.

14. Ibid., p. 19.

15. Walter Benjamin, "Central Park," trans. Lloyd Spencer, *New German Critique*, no. 34 (Winter 1985): 32–58.

16. François Dosse, "Entre histoire et memoire: Une histoire sociale de la memoire," *Raison presente* 128 (4e trimestre) (1998): 5–24.

17. Ibid., p. 9.

18. See ibid., p.13.

19. Proust, *L'Histoire*, p. 23.

20. Henri Lefebvre, *Critique of Everyday Life*, trans. John Moore (London: Verso, 1991), p. 87.

21. Proust, *L'Histoire*, p. 33.

22. The problem with Roland Barthes's pioneering attempt in his *Empire of Signs* to contest the claims of Western subjectivity by appealing to Japan's deconstructive role is that he retained the enunciative position for himself and voiced the Japanese difference, instead of actually "listening" to Japanese who already had vocalized their critique as they lived their modern transformation earlier in the century. For an account of this experience and the way the Japanese vocalized it, see H. D. Harootunian, *Overcome by Modernity: History, Culture and Community in Interwar Japan* (Princeton, NJ: Princeton University Press, 2000).

1. Tracking the Dinosaur: Area Studies in a Time of "Globalism"

1. Ruth Benedict, *The Chrysanthemum and the Sword: Patterns of Japanese Culture* (New York: Riverside Press, 1946).

2. Ravi Arvind Palat, "Fragmented Visions," unpublished manuscript, University of Hawaii, n.d., pp. 62–63.

3. Joint Committee on Japanese Studies, directed by John W. Hall, *Japanese Studies in the United States: A Report on the State of the Field—Present Resources and Future Needs* (New York: Social Science Research Council, 1970), p. 7.

4. Stanley J. Hegenbothan, "Rethinking International Scholarship," *SSRC Items* 48, nos. 2–3 (June–September 1994): 33–40.

5. William N. Fenton, *Area Studies in American Universities: For the Commission on the Implications of Armed Services Educational Programs* (Washington, DC: American Council of Learned Societies, 1947), pp. 81–82.

6. Jeffery Alexander, *Fin de Siècle Social Theory* (London: Verso, 1995), p. 11.

7. See H. D. Harootunian, "Aimai na shiruetto" (2), *Misuzu* 441, no. 5 (May 1998): 78–79.

8. Palat, "Fragmented Visions," p. 23.

9. Paul A. Cohen, *Discovering History in China* (New York: Columbia University Press, 1983).

10. See Peter Osborne, *The Politics of Time* (London: Verso, 1995), p. 18; also see Naoki Sakai, "Modernity and Its Critique: The Problem of Universalism and Particularism," in Masao Miyoshi and H. D. Harootunian, eds., *Postmodernism and Japan* (Durham, NC: Duke University Press, 1989), p. 106.

11. Palat, "Fragmented Visions," p. 34.

12. *International House of Japan Bulletin* 13, no. 1 (Winter 1993):1.

13. Joint Committee, *Japanese Studies*, pp. 32, 36.

14. Frantz Fanon, *Toward the African Revolution* (New York: Grove Press, 1967), p. 33.

15. Partha Chaterjee, *The Nation and Its Fragments: Colonial and Postcolonial Histories* (Princeton, NJ: Princeton University Press, 1993), p. 5. It should be pointed out that Chaterjee, living in a chronologically postcolonial time, was seeking to rescue "imagination" and the prior claims of an inner life that were exempted from the corrosive effects of (colonially inspired) nationalism and modern capital. This strategy recalls the discourse on the social Japanese, especially, constructed between the wars to escape the performative present in which they experienced capitalist modernization for an authentic but indeterminate past before capitalist modernization. Through the alchemy of authenticity, thinkers and writers believed they were able to change the baser metal of their present into the pure gold of an eternal experience unaffected by history.

16. Pierre Vilar, "Marxist History, History in the Making: Towards a Dialogue with Althusser," in G. Elliott, ed., *Althusser: A Critical Reader* (Oxford: Blackwell, 1994), pp. 10–43.

17. Frantz Fanon, *The Wretched of the Earth* (New York: Grove Press, 1968), p. 233.

18. Robert Young, *White Mythologies* (London: Routledge, 1990), p. 174. Young and others argue that Bhabha and Spivak seek criticism by "exploiting" the indeterminancies within rationalism itself, whereas Said and Fanon proceed from experience and consciousness. In her

recent book, *Critique of Postcolonial Reason,* Gayatri Spivak pursues this program which, unfortunately, suffers from her propensity for self-interruption and constant self-referral. The average number of pronouns indicating the "I" on any randomly selected page suggests that her critique owes more to experience and consciousness than she has admitted.

19. Aijaz Ahmad, "Postcolonialism: What's in a Name?" in Roman DeLaCampa, E. Ann Kaplan, and Michael Sprinker, eds., *Late Imperial Culture* (London: Verso, 1995), p. 31.

20. L. Grossberg, C. Nelson, and P. A. Treicher, eds., *Cultural Studies* (New York: Routledge, 1992), p. 476. Meagen Morris rightly observes that in a volume of more than seven hundred pages mapping out cultural studies, large parts of Asia, Africa, and Latin America are absent. In fact, it is astonishing, if not a Herculean feat, how a volume of such size and scale, dedicated to the catholic promises of cultural studies, could have so consistently ignored the very world which the new "discipline" supposedly occupies

21. Slavoj Žižek, *Tarrying with the Negative* (Durham, NC: Duke University Press, 1993), p. 216.

22. Homi Bhabha, *The Location of Culture* (London: Routledge, 1994), pp. 242, 245.

23. The idea is from Osborne, *The Politics of Time,* p. 190.

24. Henri Lefebvre, *Everyday Life in the Modern World* (New Brunswick, NJ: Transactions Publishers, 1994), p. 24.

25. Ibid., pp. 25, 18.

26. Osborne, *The Politics of Time,* p. 196.

27. Fredric Jameson, "On Cultural Studies," in John Rajchman, ed., *The Identity in Question* (London: Routledge, 1995), pp. 253, 264.

28. Osborne, *The Politics of Time,* p. 200.

2. The "Mystery of the Everyday": Everydayness in History

1. Homi Bhabha, *The Location of Culture* (London: Routledge, 1994), p. 86.

2. Peter Osborne, *The Politics of Time* (London: Verso, 1995), p. 2.

3. Ibid., p. xi.

4. I am opposed to more fashionable descriptions, such as "alternative modernities," "divergent modernities," "competing modernities," and "retroactive modernities," that imply the existence of an "original" that was formulated in the "West" followed by a series of "copies" and lesser inflections. The problem with these conceptions of modernity is that they are based on transmuting a temporal lag into a qualitative difference (the myth of the time lag). Moreover, they presuppose an impossible unity called the "West" and thus a unified experience empowered to override all local differences. This is precisely the kind of "spirit" Husserl constructed when he identified Europe with Greek philosophy in the 1930s. See Edmund Husserl, *The Crisis of the European Sciences*, trans. David Carr (Evanston, IL: Northwestern University Press, 1970), pp. 269–299.

5. Anthony Giddens, *The Consequences of Modernity* (Stanford, CA: Stanford University Press, 1990), pp. 18, 19.

6. Alf Ludtke, *The History of Everyday Life* (Princeton, NJ: Princeton University Press, 1995), esp. pp. 3–40, 116–148, 169–197. See also Berliner Geschictswersatt (Hersg.), *Alltagskultur, Subjektivitat und Geschicte* (Munster: Verlag Westfallisches Dampfoot, 1994).

7. Dorothy Smith, *The Everyday as Problematic* (Boston: Northeastern University Press, 1987).

8. Antonio Gramsci, *Prison Notebooks*, trans. Joseph Buttigieg (New York: Columbia University Press, 1996), vol. 2, p. 17.

9. Ōya Sōichi, "Modan sō to modan sō," *Ōya Sōichi zenshū* (Tokyo: Soyosha, 1929), vol. 2.

10. Arno Mayer, *The Persistence of the Old Regime* (New York: Pantheon Press, 1981).

11. Siegfried Kracauer, *The Mass Ornament*, trans., ed., and with an introduction by Thomas Levine (Cambridge, MA: Harvard University Press, 1995), pp. 43–44. (Cited in the text as *MO*.)

12. *Teihon Yanagita Kunio zenshū* (Tokyo: Chikuma shobō, 1968–1971), vol. 16, p. 28.

13. John Roberts, *The Art of Interruption* (Manchester: Manchester University Press, 1998), pp. 14–15.

14. Sigmund Freud, *The Pathology of Everyday Life*, trans. A. A. Brill (New York: Mentor Books, n.d.).

15. Roberts, *The Art of Interruption*, p. 16.

16. Adrian Rifkin, *Street Noises* (Manchester: Manchester University Press, 1993).

17. Kristin Ross, *Fast Cars, Clean Bodies* (Cambridge, MA: MIT Press, 1995).

18. Michael Dutton, *Street Life China* (Cambridge: Cambridge University Press, 1998).

19. Siegfried Kracauer, *Die Angestellten* (Allensbach: Verlag für Demoskopie, 1929), pp. 49–50. (Cited in the text as A); also see Siegfried Kracauer, *The Salaried Masses*, trans. Quintin Hoare and with an introduction by Inka Mulder-Bach (London: Verso, 1998), p. 62. (Cited in the text as SM.)

20. David Frisby, *Fragments of Modernity* (Cambridge, MA: MIT Press, 1986), pp. 6–7.

21. Kracauer, *Die Angestellten*, p. xix.

22. Georg Lukacs, *History and Class Consciousness*, trans. Rodney Livingstone (London: Merlin Press, 1971), p. 172.

23. Osborne, *The Politics of Time*, p. 197.

24. Lukacs, *History and Class Consciousness*, p. 192.

25. Georg Simmel, *The Philosophy of Money*, trans. Tom Bottomore and David Frisby (Boston: Routledge & Kegan Paul, 1978), p. 128. (Cited in the text as PM.)

26. Quoted in Frisby, *Fragments of Modernity*, p. 63.

27. Georg Simmel, *On Individuality and Social Forms*, ed. D. Levine (Chicago: University of Chicago Press, 1971), p. 230. (Cited in the text as GS.)

28. Lukacs, *History and Class Consciousness*, pp. 156–157.

29. Quoted in Frisby, *Fragments of Modernity*, p. 99.

30. Roberts, *The Art of Interruption*, p. 16.

31. See Leon Trotsky, *Problems of Everyday Life* (New York: Monad Press, 1979). It is interesting to see how Gramsci read this work concerning the status of *byt*—everyday life and Trotsky's "interest in Americanism" (Gramsci, *Prison Notebooks*, p. 215).

32. Roberts, *The Art of Interruption*, p. 18.

33. See H. D. Harootunian, *Overcome by Modernity: History, Culture and Community in Interwar Japan* (Princeton, NJ: Princeton University Press, 2000), chap. 3.

34. Boris Arvatov, "Everyday Life and the Culture of the Thing," trans. Christina Kiaer, *October* 81 (Summer 1997): 119–128. (Cited in the text as Arvatov.)

35. Christina Kiaer, "Boris Arbatov's Socialist Objects," *October* 81 (Summer 1997): 105.

36. I have found useful Svetlana Boym, *Common Places* (Cambridge, MA: Harvard University Press, 1994), esp. pp. 1–120, where she explains the historical meanings associated with *byt*.

37. Siegfried Kracauer, *History: The Last Things Before the Last* (Princeton, NJ: Marcus Weiner, 1995), p. 4.

38. Ibid.

39. See Frisby, *Fragments of Modernity*, p. 183, who proposes that this sense of "homelessness" resembled Lukacs's earlier articulation of the "transcendental homelessness" of *The Theory of the Novel*.

40. Frisby, *Fragments of Modernity*, p. 120.

41. Ibid.

42. Quoted in ibid., p. 125.

43. Martin Heidegger, *Being and Time*, trans. John Macquarrie and Edward Robinson (New York: Harper San Francisco, 1962). (Cited in the text as *BT*.)

44. Theodore Adorno, *The Jargon of Authenticity*, trans. Knut Tarnowski and Frederic Will (Evanston, IL: Northwestern University Press, 1973), p. 104.

45. Walter Benjamin, *Selected Writings*, ed. Marcus Bullock and Michael Jennings (Cambridge, MA: Harvard University Press, 1996), vol. 1, p. 110.

46. See Françoise Proust, *L'Histoire á contretemps* (Paris: Les éditions du Cerf, 1994), p. 30.

47. Walter Benjamin, *Paris capitale du xix siäcle: Le livre des passages*, trans. Jean LaCoste after the original edition established by Rolf Tiedemann (Paris: Les editions du Cerf, 1989), pp. 479–480 (N3,1). (Cited in the text as *Passages*.)

48. Proust, *L'Histoire*, p. 27.

49. Walter Benjamin, "Edward Fuchs: Collector and Historian," in *The Essential Frankfort School Reader*, edited and with an introduction by Andrew Arato and Eike Gebhardt (New York: Urizen Books, 1978), p. 227.

50. Walter Benjamin, "Central Park," trans. Lloyd Spencer, *New German Critique*, no. 34 (Winter 1985): 48.

51. Osborne, *The Politics of Time*, pp. 114, 116.

52. Walter Benjamin, *Charles Baudelaire: A Lyric Poet in the Era of High Capitalism*, trans. Harry Zohn (London: Verso, 1983), p. 113.

53. Karl Marx, *Capital* (New York: International Publishers, 1972), vol. 1, pp. 76, 79.

54. Walter Benjamin, *Selected Works* (Cambridge, MA: Harvard University Press, 1999), vol. 2, p. 209. See also Osborne, *The Politics of Time*, p. 182.

55. Benjamin, *Selected Works* (Cambridge, MA: Harvard University Press, 1996), vol. 1, p. 444.

56. Benjamin, *Selected Works*, vol. 2, p. 216.

57. Osborne, *The Politics of Time*, p. 185.

58. Henri Lefebvre, *Critique of Everyday Life*, trans. John Moore (London: Verso, 1991), pp. 124–125.

59. Henri Lefebvre, *Everyday Life in the Modern World*, trans. Sacha Rabinovitch (New York: Harper Torchbooks, 1971), p. 25. Also see Henri Lefebvre, *Introduction to Modernity*, trans. John Moore (London: Verso, 1995), p. 237, in which modernity, as the ghost of revolution, is abolished and the residue, which is everydayness, is now identified with uneven development.

60. Lefebvre, *Everyday Life*, pp. 18, 19, 24, 25.

61. Osborne, *The Politics of Time*, p. 196.

3. "Dialectical Optics": History in Everydayness

1. Henri Lefebvre, *Critique of Everyday Life*, trans. John Moore (London: Verso, 1991), p. 30.

2. Walter Benjamin, *Charles Baudelaire: A Lyric Poet in the Era of High Capitalism*, trans. Harry Zohn (London: Verso, 1983), p. 171.

3. Peter Osborne, *The Politics of Time* (London: Verso, 1995), pp. 187, 189.

4. Yanagita Kunio, *Meiji Taishōshi, sesōhen* (Tokyo: Kōdansha, 1993), p. 172.

5. *Hirabayashi Hatsunosuke bungei hyōron zenshū* (Tokyo: Kyōbundo, 1975), vol. 3, pp. 776–778.

6. Minami Hiroshi, ed., *Taishō bunka* (Tokyo: Keikusa shobō, 1967), pp. 246–255.

7. Terade Koji, *Seikatsu bunkaron e no shōtai* (Tokyo: Kyōbundo, 1994), p. 92.

8. *Gonda Yasunosuke chosakushū* (Tokyo: Bunwa shobō, 1974–1975), vol. 2, p. 242.

9. Kawakami Tetsutarō and Takeuchi Yoshimi, *Kindai no chōkoku* (Tokyo: Fuzambō, 1979), pp. 254–255.

10. In Yamamoto Akira, "Shakai seikatsu to henka to taishū bunka," in Iwanami kōza, *Nihon rekishi* (Tokyo: Iwanami shoten, 1976), vol. 19, p. 328.

11. Junichirō Tanizaki, *Naomi*, trans. and with an introduction by Anthony Chambers (New York: North Point Press, 1998), p. 4.

12. Minami Hiroshi, ed., *Nihon modanizumu no kenkyū* (Tokyo: Bureen shuppan, 1982), p. 26.

13. Ibid., p. 24.

14. Kon Wajirō, "Gendai fūzoku," in Nakamura Kōya, *Nihon fūzokushi kōza* (Tokyo: Yusankaku, 1929), vol. 3, p. 4. (Cited in the text as Fuzoku.) See also Miriam Silverberg, "Constructing the Japanese Ethnography of Modernity," *Journal of Asian Studies* 51, no. 1 (February 1992): 30–42.

15. Kawazoe Noboru, *Kon Wajirō*, in *Nihon minzoku bunka taikei* (Tokyo: Kōdansha, 1978), vol. 7, pp. 244–245. Kawazoe argues that Kon felt the necessity of "stopping" the rapid movement of custom in order to catch hold of it in research.

16. *Kon Wajirōshū* (Tokyo: Domesu, 1986), vol. 1, pp. 53–108. (Cited in the text as KWS.)

17. Yoshimi Shunya, *Toshi no doramatourugi* (Tokyo: Kyōbundo, 1995), p. 62.

18. *Kon Wajirōshū* (Tokyo: Domesu, 1986), vol. 5, p. 343.

19. Aono Suekichi, *Sarariman kyōfu jidai* (Tokyo: Senshinsha, 1930). (Cited in the text as Aono.)

20. It should perhaps be repeated that Kon's enthusiasm for rationalization blinded him to the problems it caused. Since the attainment of rationality represented for him the third and last stage in an evolutionary process that had led Japan out of feudal custom, he was less concerned with the contradictions it was generating and the unevenness it was producing than its possibilities for consumption and subject formation.

21. Ernst Bloch, *Heritage of Our Time*, trans. Neville Plaice and Stephen Plaice (Berkeley and Los Angeles: University of California Press, 1990), pp. 108–109.

22. See Aono Suekichi, "Geijitsu no kakumei to kakumei no geijitsu," in Kano Masanao, ed., *Taishō shisō*, vol. 2: *Kindai Nihon shisō*

taikei (Tokyo: Chikuma shobō, 1977), vol. 34, p. 234, for an account of this bourgeois "historical spirit," a product of idealism, that presumes eternality, "an ideal of the eternal" that cannot be transcended.

23. Benjamin, *Charles Baudelaire*, pp. 110–111.

24. Lefebvre, *Critique of Everyday Life*, p. 13.

25. *Tosaka Jun zenshū* (Tokyo: Keikusa shobō, 1977), vol. 4, p. 162. (Cited in the text as *TSZ*.)

26. Tosaka Jun, "Fūzoku no kōsai," in *Tosaka Jun senshū* (Tokyo: Ito shoten, 1948), p. 4. (Cited in the text as *TJS*.)

27. Marilyn Ivy, *Discourses of the Vanishing* (Chicago: University of Chicago Press, 1995), p. 56.

28. Paul Anderer, *Literature of the Lost Home* (Stanford, CA: Stanford University Press, 1995), p. 79. (Kobayashi, "Discourse on the Fiction of the Self")

29. Yoshimoto Takaaki, ed., *Kobayashi Hideo shū* (Tokyo: Chikuma shobō, 1977), pp. 221, 223, 231. (Cited in the text as *KHS*.)

30. Alice Kaplan and Kristin Ross, eds., *Everyday Life*, in *Yale French Studies*, no. 73 (New Haven, CT: Yale University Press, 1987), p. 15.

INDEX

ACLS. *See* American Council
of Learned Societies
actuality, 147, 150, 154; of every-
dayness, 1–24, 151
Adorno, Theodor, 41, 85, 98
advertising, 117–18, 123
Africa, 9, 38, 48, 51, 59, 162n20
Ahmad, Aijaz, 52
Algeria, 70
Althusser, Louis, 45
American Council of Learned
Societies (ACLS), 30, 32
Americanism, 66–67, 68, 82, 84,
119, 164n31
Americanization, 89–90. *See
also* United States
Anderson, Benedict, 16
Andō Nobuyoshi, 145
Die Angestellten (Kracauer), 71,
85, 87, 89, 91, 94, 117
Ankersmit, Frank, 10
Anti-Oedipus (DeLeuze and
Guattari), 53
Aono Suekichi, 83, 91, 124; on
salaryman class, 91–92, 122–
23, 125, 133–40
Arbatov, Boris, 21, 66, 67, 78–
85, 127
area studies, 25–58; as anachro-
nism, 28–29; in Association
of Asian Studies, 26–27;
and business interests, 29,
30, 31, 46; and censorship,

30, 43; and cold war, 29,
31, 32, 33, 34; and cultural
studies, 22, 41, 45–47, 58;
East-West dichotomy in,
25–28; and ethnicity, 34–35;
fieldwork in, 38–40; funding for, 27, 30–31, 32,
35–36, 42, 43–45, 52–53;
and history, 32–33; motives
for, 36, 38; and nation-
states, 32, 36, 41, 42, 46;
periodic surveys of, 42–43;
and power, 45–46; theory
in, 39–40, 42, 52, 61; in
universities, 29–32, 44–45;
and Vietnam War, 29, 31,
34; and World War II, 30
"Area Studies in American Universities" (Fenton), 32
art, 1, 13; Benjamin on, 108;
bourgeois, 80; and every-
dayness, 79, 132, 152, 155;
and history, 11, 12; performance, 156–57; and produc-
tion, 78–80, 84
Art and Production (Arbatov),
79
Asia, 5, 66, 162n20; colonialism
in, 51, 59; as "field," 38;
historiography of, 6, 9; as
phantom, 25, 57; study of,
6–7, 25–28. *See also particular countries*